UNLOCKING YOUR VOICE:

FREEDOM TO SING

by

ESTHER SALAMAN

With a Foreword by
Mark Elder

KAHN & AVERILL

LONDON

S0-BMW-756

This second edition first published in 1999 by
Kahn & Averill
9 Harrington Road, London SW7 3ES

Reprinted 2000, 2004

First edition published in 1989 by
Victor Gollancz Ltd, London

Copyright © 1989 & 1999 by Esther Salaman

The right of Esther Salaman to be identified as the
author of this work has been asserted by her in accor-
dance with the Copyright, Design and Patents Act 1988

All rights reserved

British Library Cataloguing in Publication Data
A catalogue record for this book is available
from the British Library

ISBN 1 871082 70 6

Printed in Great Britain by
Halstan & Co Ltd, Amersham, Bucks

PREFACE TO SECOND EDITION

IT IS OVER ten years since I began to gather my thoughts for the first edition of this book, and many more years since I felt impelled to think, teach, talk and write about a way of encouraging the singing voice – ideas which I wanted to share with others.

In this edition I have tried to produce a little more order than before. I still repeat myself a good deal, rather as one does in teaching, with different slants on the same ideas, and I hope this proves to be, not an irritant but a source of helpful reinforcement. I have also added some limbering-up exercises that have a special bearing on the process of 'unlocking your voice' and giving singers the freedom to sing.

Anatomy is little dealt with: others have researched into and explained the science of our amazing vocal machinery, which nevertheless still has its mysteries. I try, in these pages, to describe the *sensations* of the singing voice in action – which do not always tally with the workings of the anatomy – and to suggest the astonishing responses that our emotions can elicit from technique, at every stage.

This is the domain I explore and its myriad pathways are the landscape through which I hope you will journey with me. Sometimes we may feel that we are treading on shifting sands and only now and then do we feel secure. But it is an adventure with great rewards.

E.S.

ACKNOWLEDGEMENTS

Acknowledgement is due to the following for material quoted in the text: A. & C. Black for quotations from *The Foundations of Singing* by Franklyn Kelsey published by Williams & Norgate in 1950; The Oxford University Press for quotations from *The Gentle Art of Singing*, 1930, by Sir Henry Wood; The Oxford University Press and Lucie Manén for a quotation from *The Art of Singing* by Lucie Manén (originally published by Faber & Faber, 1974, now revised and updated under the title *Bel Canto* and published by the Oxford University Press, 1987).

My warmest thanks to Lynore McWhirter for demonstrating various dos and don'ts of singing positions and to Dr Harold Rose who photographed them. To Mark Elder for his Foreword, to my dear friends Alison Truefitt and Elizabeth Clough for their unfailing encouragement and support, to my children, Peter and Nina, and Margaret Dain for her proof-reading of the second edition – not forgetting the many singers of every age and stage who taught me so much during out years of mutual discovery.

E.S.

AUTHOR'S NOTE

In the exercises which accompany the text of this book, the vowels 'a', 'e', 'i', 'o' and 'u' (oo) should be pronounced as if in the Italian language. English words that give equivalent sounds are shown on p. 59.

The pronouns 'he' and 'she' are used throughout the book when discussing a pupil or singer; in almost all cases they should be considered interchangeable.

References to pitch in the text and exercises apply to the middle octave of the singer's voice. Where pitch is crucial the Helmholz notation is used.

15th June, 1992.

Dear Madame Salaman,

   Thank you so much for your "little book" which I am finding quite fascinating as you make statement after statement which please and flatter my own comprehension of the art of singing! I am not over-fond of speaking too physiologically regarding the actual emission of sound as it is actually a reflex, but it seems to me that many young singers just don't have a clue about breathing, supporting and projecting! They are musically very proficient but have not the vocal technique to carry off the simplest aria, let alone the difficult ones they usually present!

   My compliments, and I hope you will have lots of readers -- who heed your words.

     Sincerely,

     Joan Sutherland
      O.M., A.C., D.B.E.

CONTENTS

Foreword by Mark Elder

Prelude   1

Unlocking Your Voice   13

The Start of the Note and Vowel Centering   21

Freedom and Agility   27

Vibrazione – Vibrancy   33

Messa di Voce – Expression: Dynamics   38

Resonance   46

'Covering the Sound' and Registers   51

Your Daily Voice Limbering   56

Vowels and Consonants   59

The Wish to Sing   63

Tension and Performance   66

Voice Strain and Other Hazards   79

The Pleasures and Perils of the Singing Profession   86

Side Tracks and Deception   93

Teachers and Students   97

More About Bel Canto   116

Choir Trainers   122

Finale   126

Appendix: Analysis of Schubert's 'An die Musik'   133

FOREWORD

by Mark Elder

WE ALL SING somehow or other. For some of us, it happens in the flattering acoustic of the shower, for others the enveloping effect of a large choir or choral society is what excites us; a few of us find ourselves on the stages of the world's opera houses.

Esther Salaman's little book is designed to appeal in differing degrees to us all. It is written by someone who has a lifetime of teaching behind her and considerable first-hand experience of the trials and tribulations of the profession. Indeed, her candour over her own struggles as a soloist is rare, and must surely help to recommend her understanding and compassion to the struggling singer, whether amateur or professional. She goes straight to the heart of the matter, and succeeds in making something often so elusive and mysterious seem easily within our grasp. She certainly 'unlocks' the problems!

The discussions relating to the Bel Canto technique will particularly interest the professional, and the chapters on the wider issues of singing will, I am sure, appeal to everyone who 'aspires to sing'! Whether in private lessons or master classes, Salaman's skill is well-known. In particular, her work each year at the Dartington Summer School reveals the enormous enjoyment that can be gained from an open-hearted (and -throated) approach to singing.

In this book, she encapsulates very pithily the basis of her teaching methods, and I feel sure it will be welcomed, by singers and teachers alike, for its directness and sound common-sense.

PRELUDE

MOST OF US who aspire to sing, at whatever level, long to *unlock* our voices — to find a way to express sounds in music and words communicating feeling that we cannot express in other ways. When this begins to happen there is a great sense of freedom; of physical and emotional well-being. When we hear great singers we instantly feel the impact of their 'unlocked' sounds and emotion carried directly and buoyantly to us, and our response is immediate.

But too often, both in speech and singing, we are not fully committed to the sounds we make — either emotionally or 'technically' — except perhaps when caught unawares in moments of joy or anger, or other unexpected emotions. We may even *hide* behind our communications, and present a contrived or impersonal voice to the world.

We British are, I think, particularly poor at communicating our sound. There is a national reticence, a shyness; and the 'stiff upper lip' may literally be stiff! Our English language has mixed vowels and dipthongs, awkward to negotiate, which can lessen the impact of our talking. But there are ways of managing our language, which, at its best, can be wonderfully expressive and subtle: what matters is the *commitment* in the words by whoever is expressing them. At whatever stage we are, I do believe we could all do better — open up and dare a little more.

However, I believe, ever more certainly, that there is only *one basic way* of finding our best sound, of getting our energy together and allowing it to ring out in the pleasure of communication: Nature's way, as endorsed by the lusty screaming of a four-month-old baby, and by the only long-surviving school of singing there has ever been — the Italian Bel Canto school.

Think about a healthy four-month-old baby, lying on his back, *yelling*. His entire position is a lesson in voice technique: shoulders back, chest expanded, tummy in, and throat wide open. He seems to gain strength as he screams. He does not tire — only the grown-ups who hear the noise do that. Nor does his ear-splitting sound deteriorate in quality. Nature seems to say to that baby: 'Keep at it! Enjoy yourself! You'll get what you want, and you'll frighten the adults, and you'll grow stronger every moment ... *and* you'll feel drunk with your own sound.' Does the operatic tenor feel rather the same when his exhilarating top Cs ring out? To recapture this vocal position in later life can be a positively rejuvenating exercise — not for beauty, but for muscular strengthening of the larynx, which later can make for beauty. Variations of this sound are used by non-singing adults only for very special purposes, such as selling newspapers in the streets. Or perhaps, sadly, only when drunk enough to risk it, or for calling across great distances out of doors. This muscular position of 'supported yelling' has been well developed in the Music Theatre world and is a much-used sound known as Belting. It needs tackling with know-how. It is included most carefully into the remarkable system of skills devised by Joe Estill in her 'Voicecraft with Compulsory Figures'. No damage is done to the 'perpetrator' of these sounds because their bodies are properly and *wholly* involved as with the healthy baby. A *total muscularity* is used ... particularly around collar-bone and chest as well as lower back and tummy — all well braced.

There are moments in the skilled opera singer's 'palette'

of sounds and colours when these same skills are *briefly* used to meet great emotion and power.

Do not experiment without supervision or tuition!

While Nature tends to assert herself, and some singers really are 'naturals' who follow a physical instinct amounting to the very concepts which the Bel Canto school developed, many singers have to tread a harder path. I remember my own very difficult early years. As a singing student in and out of music college I was ever hopeful, dreamy and confused, maybe obtuse, certainly mystified. Again and again I seemed to 'see the light', but each time it would fade. Every two or three years I would try to work with another teacher — several were illustrious performers yet they had so little to tell. Were they inarticulate, or so instinctive in their craft that they did not know what they did, or was I unable to take suggestions at that stage?

And, another worry: whatever were those zoo animal noises perpetrated in good faith in the studios where we took our lessons? No qualifications were needed for a teacher to set up on their own in these singing studios. Frightening indeed! Things are not *so* different even today, but happily there is more discernment. And why did I persist? Earning was not pressing at that time — if it had been, would my path have become clearer? My persistence was an impelling drive, which I now understand and greatly respect as I meet it in many youngsters needing to express emotion through the voice wherever it may lead and however hard the journey.

Whatever my own shaky technique could or could not achieve, the sharing of songs in performance was a great satisfaction. I could communicate this way. My voice slid between acceptable tones, and sounds more usually connected with a diseuse or cabaret artist, while feeling myself deeply into the words and letting them lead me. In this way

I sang for years, enjoying a wide and unusual repertory, but being unable to develop the voice in quality or range; at risk technically most of the time, with nerves agonizingly taut. The results in concerts were exciting partly because of the whiff of danger in the doing of it! The performances called forth praise for compelling interpretation, or abuse for uneven tone: both were true.

In those days, after the last war when my career was beginning, singers were not on the move internationally as today, but when a great voice emerged from home or abroad it was unmistakable and our excitement was great. Recording and broadcasting skills were growing fast. Radio then tended to favour light voices; depth and intensity could not be easily contained without reduction, and so a kind of deception was transmitted. Deception was increasingly with us because of microphone techniques. In the classical vocal field deception came gradually, tastefully, insidiously. But in the pop, rock, and folk world the singer could use any sound, however meagre: near-spoken crooning, sobbing, singing or screaming. These sounds could be (and are) manipulated by the cunning of the microphone and its electronic aids to a quite shattering degree of deception which, increasingly over the last 40 years, has actually become an 'art form' of its own. It is far removed from any kind of vocal balance which is the main concern of this book. The Pop Rock sounds cause extremes of excitement initiating wild responses. As the vocalist's pitch rises, so does their public's fervour — the vocalist reaches the 'Everest' of his performance at the 'change', 'bridge' or 'passagio' of his range, and at this point makes his *own very real vocal stress* the *charge* for total emotion, showing the 'cost' in an anguished facial expression and screech and an extremely strained throat.

This way of vocalising can only take so much before burning up.

The excitement, the lifestyle, the money and the power of winding up vast young audiences must make it worth their while — ?

Although I knew no vocal security — either as a student or as a professional singer — I guessed at its existence from the feel I sometimes received in response to hearing the occasional great voice. The ring in sound communicated itself directly into my ears, head and throat. This sound had a centre to it, a heart, a kernel — and a resultant ringing resonance. Could this be the kind of 'golden thread' recalled nostalgically by certain of my elders? Certainly, I could hear this was singing as nature intended. But *how* was it done?

As the years went by, I moved wearily to my eighth teacher. An answer flashed into view. Certain very old ideas came to me as totally new. Ideas were sparked off by that brilliant researcher into vocal matters, Lucie Manén. She was then researching the great Italian school of singing begun in the seventeenth century and developed onwards: this school of ideas so vaguely termed 'Bel Canto'.

One of her first instructions knocked me back: "Do not spit or push out your notes, but imbibe the sound, 'drink' it, 'implode' not 'explode'. Fill your head with sound, become a ringing bell". I was thunderstruck. Thus began a total change in my attitude to producing sound, which I have never ceased to feel and develop. I had to learn to *sense* rather than merely *hear*. I found the 'start' or 'heart' of my voice within, at the glottis, a centre where the breath meets the vocal cords. What is more, I was allowed and encouraged to feel this happening.

Awareness of the voice-box had, before, been mysteriously taboo. This new and sensitive awareness quite naturally necessitated the spacey, resiliently open back of mouth and throat, the alert face, and the little muscles around nose and eyes awakening high resonances: in all, allowing the vocal system to unlock, enabling the larynx to do its work with no obstacles in its way. Hitherto mysterious phrases became wonderfully real: *Inhalare la voce, Chiaroscuro, Rapporto* (a true alignment of energy), and the inspired notion (of the Bel Cantists) of opening the throat and taking in breath as though suddenly and happily 'surprised' on the 'a' vowel, which stood for happiness.

Soon there unfolded the ideas and exercises for depth, intensity (not loudness), and vibrancy, the *vibrazione*, that brief moment of accented energy when the vowel sound and supported breath meet buoyantly. As Franklyn Kelsey writes in his remarkable article, 'Voice', in Grove's *Dictionary of Music and Musicians*, 5th edition, '*Vibrazione* is a tonal gesture of the larynx, correctly used the greatest voice tonic and developer of all,' And this leads to the *messa di voce*, a phrase that I had previously not understood, wondering aimlessly if it were a relative of 'mezza voce'.

Messa di voce, the system of controlling our every shade of crescendo and decrescendo in degrees of intensity, needing great athletic skill at source, and using the whole body. All this brings security, an anchor available whatever flights the voice, and music, wish to take. The buoyant support of the breath is freed, and excellent notions for managing agility fall into place — and much more. Again, Franklyn Kelsey puts it well: "It cannot be too strongly emphasized that the entire Bel Canto method is built upon the isolation of the continual 'caress of the glottis', giving this precedence over processes of breathing, of tone amplification and articulation ..." The Bel Cantists built up their school of teaching upon instinct, now endorsed by science — they learnt from the sound and action of the best natural voices around them.

Why, and when, were these health-giving essentials of the Bel Canto system lost? Maybe during the nineteenth century when the profession understandably took fright when confronted by weighty orchestral writing, and darkly dramatic and philosophical subject matter performed in large opera houses? At this time every sort of new notion was tried in attempting to increase volume — quantity rather than quality. Schools of voice production arose, teaching various placements, not maintaining the act of singing at the instrument — at source — but placing the sound in the many nooks and crannies of the head. Since this time, every slant of technique has been tried and used in amazing convolutions, and many of us have been casualties.

The Bel Canto teachers had the saying: *Cerca la qualità e la quantità verrà.* The wisdom of that sentence, telling us that quality should be established first of all and quantity will follow, constantly comes to my mind as I hear and ponder on the singing voices around us today — at every level of expertise. We hear singers who are wonderfully talented, versatile, musical and attractive, but there is nearly always a lack of balance in their sound, a bias towards quantity rather than that precious quality, or centre. We hear sounds which tend to be overloaded, tilted towards a very forward focus at the expense of that steady centre, or core, and the warmer sonorities. One feels that singers are not wholly in alignment with themselves. If a part of the totality of singing is missing, and there is an imbalance in a singer's skills, the voice still functions, but at cost and under strain, a strain not always recognized by the singer herself in the early stages. The larynx then tries hard to compensate by bearing added burdens ingeniously and gallantly. This sound is muddy — impersonal.

Talented young singers of today meet every kind of temptation. If required, they accept widely varied and challenging vocal employment: operatic roles of every weight and style; Music Theatre which expects every kind of vocal sound from shriek to speech; recitals and oratorio, and much more. Although there is not now the same kind of time span to work and grow into safe technique as in the past, I believe it to be practical and, indeed, vital that we teachers, with our various ideas, find some way of encouraging a better balance in voices: a link-up between the start or heart of the note, where it comes *from* and where it goes *to*.

Teaching young singers today, I have found it very hard to work at these notions. Students feel extremely competitive among themselves, and quantity of sound is valued over quality — or so they think. And so is speed in getting something to show: a big voice, and as soon as possible, invites notices and jobs! Young singers may be full of potential, but have no idea of what is lasting in their equipment, nor how coarseness builds up as a result of pushing the sound, when that dreaded waver or even wobble may develop and where flexibility becomes impossible. But I know very well, and very sadly from my own history, and now from being asked to help young singers as they advance in the profession and may begin to feel and show the strains. They accept readjustment or additions to their skills with relief and renewed energy. But if they do resist change, it is understandable because the familiar feels more secure than the new — the new needs to become part of their muscular memory by much repetition and time before it can be trusted.

Because of a nagging worry concerning these matters, I feel ever more strongly about the way I try to teach, hoping to re-work what I have come to believe are the essentials of the old Italian Bel Canto school without losing sight of the very different demands being made on singers today. The most daunting difference between then and now — a span of 250 years — is in the *attitude* to vocal studies. In those leisured days it is clear that the various parts of vocal technique were practised daily over *years*. Tuition was concentrated and there was much less pressure towards *immediate* prowess. A student would live in a teacher's home, maybe help in the house, listen to others, and only gradually begin to study.

In my view the singing voice comes to life *in totality* only when all those facets, so well understood by the Bel Canto teachers, come together in balance. They thus make an alignment of energy that can work naturally, and so well that students at every stage can grasp something of 'the way': for a moment feeling good, released — even elated. When it comes to working the various parts *in depth*, then great application is needed: sometimes more than a student is willing to give.

Working at the various parts of the mechanism in this way, we must never lose sight of the whole: no area excludes another, but adds to it, interacts with it, and aids the whole. In the chapters that follow, I shall describe these basic areas for work, give a few of the many vocal exercises that I use (more can always be invented or developed) to encourage these areas, and mention some of the diverse reactions to them that I meet as I teach. Detailed anatomy or precise physiological details will not be found in this book. What will be found is an indication of the 'feel' of the working of both voice and body, described in words, maybe repeated often and from various angles.

Communication in discussing our invisible instrument is very difficult, and so misunderstandings happen constantly between teacher and student, teacher and teacher, student and student. Even as I write this I am very much aware that words have different meanings and suggestions for all of us. Sometimes I cannot recognize an expression of an idea that I have suggested when it comes back to me! I was baffled by words heard from my own teachers years ago, and now I only hope I am not baffling others.

For this kind of voice production, in which I believe, and for the teaching needed to support it, the 1980s and '90s and on into the next century are now, and will be, an urgent time. We need to get to the heart of the matter because of the exceptional pressures put upon our professional singers, and because of the confusion that exists about vocal sound — amongst singers and listeners alike.

If we look at the experience of potential young singers during their school days, there exists a great deal of encouragement and opportunity for study, leading them ultimately towards the music colleges. Then there is a bottle-neck: singing students who do well understandably become *very* competitive, almost hurtling forward to get quick results and to get noticed as fast as possible. This climate encourages big voices quickly achieved. Other considerations become secondary. Students mostly steer towards opera, whether suitable or not. Concert work is scarce, and though the preparation for this — musical, interpretative and in terms of style and finesse — is indeed very well taught at advanced levels there is, sadly, little outlet for the results.

Ideally, young singers need to perform in smallish theatres and halls to encourage normal growth. The small operatic companies, both in the profession and on the 'fringe', which perform in reasonable sized venues are tremendously useful, and take up some of the great number of talented hopefuls. But our national opera houses are vast. How wonderfully better if, instead, we could have several smaller houses! This would use many more singers with much less strain on the emerging voices.

As things are, voices are pushed to their limits and beyond, attempting — and possibly succeeding — to ride full-sized, robust orchestras. At first, excitement, brute strength and verve carry the singers along, and there may be deserved acclaim. But soon the sound may become pushed, spread, hooty, over-blown, unyielding, rigid, wavery (especially at the top of the range). In short, the centre or core of the sound — and the resultant beauty — is lost. What is more, most of the public neither know what is happening nor what they are missing. They respond to the artistry and general impression of the singer, but as regards quality of sound they simply take what is on offer without complaint. However, I must add that when fine quality of sound does emerge, there is an instant positive recognition amongst the listeners which is quite physical.

Singers are gallantly giving of their best, with much energy and goodwill; but how much could be gained if the technique that I am advocating were more widely understood. It could be part of their equipment and so channel their strength into the centre, or core, of their sound. This athletic control could become an anchor, thereby freeing the whole person for more expression, colour, and varied, flexible sound.

UNLOCKING YOUR VOICE

NOW WE CAN sort out and develop your basic needs for your growing skills. The exercises call for awareness of your tools which you will wish to summon at will. Each and every skill can trigger off the rest. Eventually it must involve the whole of you — a totality.

As singers and communicators of sound we probably all agree that a certain physical bearing or stance is not only helpful but necessary: a stance that encourages us to be taller, broader, nobler and a little grander in aspect than usual. It is a *confident* stance: shoulders 'back and down' which helps swing the rib-cage forward and wide, with the breast-bone area high and broad. This confident stance discourages collapse; standing like this we will soon find a kind of comfortable 'pull-up', a connection right through from the groin area, engaging the lower tummy muscles, a chain reaction of alerted muscles *right the way up to the voice-box* — the larynx. This connection becomes our best friend — our 'support'. Help from the lower back muscles seem to support the chest area in a manner that is related to the Bel Cantist's 'appogiare la voce' — to lean the voice on to the support. I think that it is important to say that *relaxation* for singers is an overused and vague term — it does not belong to our singing needs which are more about the ease that comes through good 'spring-y' alignment. We use the word 'relax' in order to avoid stiffness, but it so easily descends into floppiness during which we 'fall apart'. So keep relaxation for moments when NOT singing — between

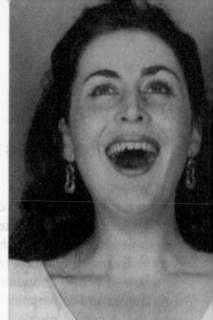

STUDENT: Is this wide-open enough?

TEACHER: Yes! It is indeed.

STUDENT: It feels good, open — free — even exultant! I would find this openness instinctively for my higher notes above the stave.

TEACHER: Yes; and the feel of space back there in your throat (the pharynx) should be available at *any* time — varying a little, and with less need for such a wide open mouth. You are looking more than happy — exultant!

phrases, before renewing and gathering strength again.

Every intake of breath is another chance to get together our alignment of energy. The breath should be taken with an open throat. The gesture should be of 'happy surprise' (not shock), as when we suddenly meet a friend, or when the sun comes out on a cloudy day. We can think of the breath-take, and the opening of the throat in readjusting to sing, as *one gesture*. The breath comes in by instinct and silently because there is nothing in its way — this gesture of 'happy surprise' sets up our entire performing frame or scaffolding. Take each breath silently through the mouth with the throat wide open and the face alert. Rather as though a light had been switched on, the alert face will help raise the soft palate which in turn enables the back of the throat to open. At once there is a feeling of space: space behind and above and at the sides of the voice-box. this *'spacey' sensation* should be available throughout our singing. Caruso felt the space in the throat to be rather square — 'like a letter box'. Others describe the feel of a 'ball of air' that must never be squashed. The bright Italian 'a', as in *'caro'*, needs the widest open position. In English this vowel is used in 'sun' and 'come' (spoken with a London accent). When a doctor asks to look at your throat in case there is inflammation or swollen tonsils he asks you to 'say ah'. It usually takes a few tries before the openness can be achieved. When finally we get it wide enough for the doctor to see — *that* is the position that the singer needs much of the time — not exaggerated, not a grimace.

Here are some detailed exercises to help stance and warming up sounds.

1. Sitting tall on an upright chair:
   Curl up into a 'ball', head towards lap, as small as you can — then un-curl slowly, steadily, feeling the back of your chair until you are again sitting tall.
   Legs, knees, squarely planted on ground — sitting tall.
   Now allow your head to roll gently, beginning by dropping head forward and roll around, but only *half*-way around, then gently drop it forward again and roll it around the other half-way — and finally drop forward again — and back to normal.

2. Still sitting; wriggle your face and with your fingers, massage around eyes and cheeks toward ears and enjoy grimacing — including chewing movements.

3. Now try some light humming (any pitch) in your own easy-going way.

4. Now swing your weight forward, and as your legs are well placed, one good swing forward will take you up into a standing position — stand tall and proud, feeling your strength around the collar bone which should be braced.

5. Roll both shoulders, simultaneously, over, back and down in one continuous movement; with a feeling of a continuous circle; your shoulder-blades may crunch together a little! Keep breathing easily.

6. For a moment just stand quietly feeling good; then make a little sound of a rolled 'RRR' (and if you really cannot roll your 'Rs' then a sound like 'FFT' would do) 2 or 3 times with one hand lightly on top of your chest and feel a rise in response to the sound. Now a hand to the base of your tummy and feel a similar movement rising to meet the sound; and try a hand on the side of your rib cage — quite high, and again there will be a slight response.

7. Now let everything go: your face, your body, your knees; let all breath out — shake yourself like a rag doll — then when you feel ready, swing both your arms right up, reaching tall and 'basket' hands (palms up, fingers twined) as you stretch even more, taking breath spontaneously as you swing up.

Now the hard part. Bring the arms *outstretched sideways down* as *slowly* as you can together with an equally *slow exhalation*, with teeth and jaw closed and with the sound 'FFF', feeling a big resistance to the breath. This resistance in *singing* would be *at* the vocal folds — with this exhalation you can feel the involvement of your *whole being*. If you do this exercise twice with a moment of rest between, you will feel invigorated and rather virtuous!

As we open our throats to take every breath as though happily surprised, this resilient alignment, an alignment of energies, can be felt supported at its roots like a squeeze 'in and up' standing tall, a mild expression of pleased surprise — 'ah!' — produces this muscular response. Caruso said that he felt his stomach and buttocks were trying to *meet* as he sang! Most of us are lucky to feel *some* kind of gentle buoyancy which we can renew and which brings energy, controlling our steady breath pressure. Working in this way, we can leave our diaphragm muscles free to do their own excellent job without special attention. Never try to concentrate on what you think is your diaphragm — in fact it cannot be felt. You can, however, feel the breadth of the rib-cage and the braced area of the breast-bone, from whence a good deal of valuable resonance springs, as support is maintained.

In a general sense we can feel *breadth* as we inhale and *lift* as we launch our sound. Some singing teachers prefer thinking of the intake of breath as being through the nose: yes, if the nostrils are alert and flared, the throat open, the intake will be silent and equally good, though slower than through the mouth. The breath-taking gesture, the 'happy surprise' is rather similar to a conductor's up-beat . . . or the

This a comfortable stance through which the voice system is free to do what the mind and imagination suggest — a natural alignment of energy

And here our singer is deliberately getting it wrong — off balance — stressful . . .

dancers 'and ... one, two, three ... '. Above all, it is a total alertness.

Although this book has no anatomical explanations for all we do and feel in our singing endeavours, I have always wanted to visualise where my vocal folds reside, as so much — indeed all — depends on their function. They are unfeelable, except when badly inflamed, or very gently and briefly at the onset of a vowel sound.

If you have occasion to look through a Fibreopticscope at this area of the throat you will still find it hard to believe that you are the owner of such a vocal arrangement!

At the top of our windpipe within the larynx (behind the 'Adams Apple') there is a kind of 'drumhead' cover with a slit along the middle from front to back. The edges of this slit are the *True vocal folds*, their precise length, thickness and variations of closure are all important. They have very many muscles and possibilities. Over the top and sides of them are the *False vocal folds*, quite thick and 'sausage-like' in shape, whose task is to protect the windpipe by closing over the true vocal folds and preventing morsels of food or drink going the wrong way and when tightly closed they prevent any movement of breath in or out. You can feel this closure when you need to lift something very heavy! TRY! As singers we are interested in the ability to draw back the false vocal folds — rather like parting curtains! They also contribute to the lubrication of the *True folds*. For the purposes of normal breathing and for speech they draw back or 'retract' as needed. For singing, particularly when using the entire range, they need to retract greatly. For a clear quality of sound that we wish to use in classical singing we have to work on their efficient retraction *continuously*! That is what our main vocal effort is about.

All the exercises about opening the throat: the 'Happy

Surprise', the retraction, the sensation of drinking or inner
laughter, the 'inhalare la voce', the 'siren' and more, are all
directed towards the elasticity and efficiency of this retraction which encourages vigorous and athletic behaviour of
the *True vocal folds* — and a clear true sound.

Very basically, the 'drumhead', the top of the windpipe,
is rather like this, looking down:

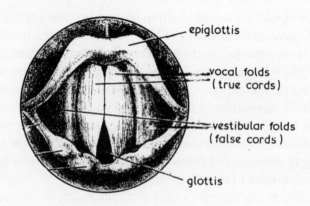

epiglottis

vocal folds
(true cords)

vestibular folds
(false cords)

glottis

THE START OF THE NOTE AND
VOWEL CENTERING

Let us find the actual starting place of the sound, the birth of the vowel, at source. The researchers of the Bel Canto school, who explored and gathered wisdom over about 200 years, advocated the forming of vowels 'inwardly' at the level of the glottis, i.e. the vocal cords, or 'folds', where breath turns into sound. Apart from ventriloquists, most of us, in this country at least, are used to forming vowels at mouth level, as practised in speech (and in 'elocution', often to the detriment of the sound, causing it to 'flatten out') and to disconnect from the alignment.

This is the correct onset for classical singing and I think the basis for all our technical work. Let the feel of this start of your sound 'stay' with your singing whatever other skills are constantly drawn in as you proceed.

In this connection and to digress; I was so happy about a meeting with Dame Joan Sutherland in the summer of 1997. She was opening the International Conference in London concerning the teaching of singing. Dame Joan's first words to me recalled the 'Happy Surprise' (described in my book) which she told me that she constantly uses herself and shares with others. As she talked it did indeed seem part of her lively, warm, expressive appearance!

One can soon learn to feel the *place* where sound starts; also the area where the vowel is formed. The most basic Bel Canto exercise was about precisely this, the *onset* of the note. The exercise draws attention to the tiny 'click' that accompanies the meeting of breath and vocal cords. The back of the mouth and throat need to be wide open allowing the mechanism freedom to work. One should feel the onset of the note more as an *implosion* than an explosion of breath. Do not be afraid of a new awareness in this area. Quality of tone depends on air compression and resistance in good balance. For this our diaphragm needs liberty to ascend — it takes this liberty quite naturally without your special attention. The Bel Cantists felt their throats to be their mouths! There are more spaces in there than you have thought about! A feel of 'drinking' reveals this. The more we feel the elasticity of the spaces behind and at the sides of the voice-box, the better our marvellous vocal machine, the larynx, with its many muscles, can work for us; and the more space and elasticity, the more precision our vocal cords will give us. You will soon experience the feeling as you try the exercises below. We need to have this experience of where our voices are coming *from* as well as where they are going *to*. For soon the feeling becomes a control, a *security* which we can use to vary the intensity of our singing according to the dynamic and emotional demands of the moment. We can also afford to forget about it, and to find it again as we wish.

Exercises for the Start of the Note and Vowel Centering
Let us try this:- preparing for it with the 'Happy Surprise' on the first rest.

The Start of the Note

on one supported breath.

The quaver rest before beginning this exercise is the 'Happy Surprise' or the alert switch! A silent breath is automatically taken which will last for the whole exercise: the further rests can be felt as a preparation for the onset of the next note — ('the caress of the glottis').

You can also try this 'feel' of where the sound happens *un*sung, just feeling the tiny click.

With your good stance: alert face, open throat and 'Happy Surprise' silent breath — just touch these five notes up and down, feeling the place where the sound 'happens' (at the glottis). It will feel like a tiny click. Make each tiny sound as though *imploding*, not pushing or exploding. When you have found the feeling of implosion, sing a triad-plus-one on vowels:

Vowel Centering

Start carefully as in the start-of-the-note exercise, then centre into the vowels — let it be quite legato or even 'slurry'.

The 'gesture' of the 'Happy Surprise' is best found by *acting it out* rather than *puzzling* it out technically — a simple quick action, which automatically includes a silent intake of breath. Remember the gesture is *happy*, not a 'shocked' surprise, which does not open the throat in the same way. Acting out 'silent laughter' also has a good effect.

Having done this, extend the gesture into light happy imploded sounds on 'a' and any of the other open vowels — e, i, o, oo — all on the one breath.

Be free with your arms and change your weight from side to side if you wish. Now pitch a note mid-voice and try the same gesture of 'Happy Surprise', followed by a legato line of all five vowels giving the vowels clear definition made from 'within' rather than with mouth changes.

Now try the same open-throated 'a' for the triad-plus-one, and allow each of the three vowels to be uttered *inwardly* at the same place as you have located and felt the start of the note. The line of the vowel sound is continuous, and the feel is more of *drinking* at the back of the throat than of pushing sound out. Feel that there is more space *behind* and around the sound.

Now we can try some slightly more extended shapes: the vowels should be clear and defined within the legato line

or on any vowels of your choice

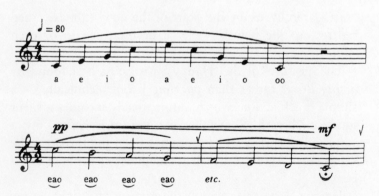

Try these vowels, well differentiated, on each note

eao   etc.

This scale should gather intensity into the vowels as you proceed; the 'e' should help brighten the other two vowels. Also sing on one vowel alone: 'i', 'e', at lower pitches; 'o', 'a', at higher pitches. Take the breath as indicated. Do not be tempted to do without! The five vowels we are using are: a, e, i, o, u as in the Italian: am*a*to, ved*e*re, Mar*i*a, t'ad*o*ro, fort*u*na.

Useful English equivalents (in a London accent) are:
'a' as in sun
'e' as in yes
'i' as in sing
'o' as in not
'oo' (u) as in moon
Always be careful not to squeeze the 'i' into a shrill 'ee', but rather think of it as in 'sing'.

With your thoughts, open all available spaces around, beneath and above the voice-box. You will then free and alert the muscles that take care of the required action of the vocal folds. You cannot hurt these muscles by using them.

Make friends with the feel of the start, the *onset* of your sound. Later you can call upon this same place for more control when you need added depth and intensity.

This needs more inner energy than you might think, and even more so as you go higher through the changing or 'passagio' notes. Please don't be alarmed: stay with the effort of more inner energy into each vowel up to F or F# — your 'support' muscles will respond to your needs.

Now back to your middle starting note and continue the exercises: taking it carefully down step by step over the 'lower passagio' between F and C, which also needs considerable energy, and as you reach middle C (an octave lower for men) you may need to incorporate a *mixture* of sound; near speech, bring warmth to your sound without a sudden change into 'chest voice' — keep your 'alert' muscles lively in your countenance all the time, and nothing will go wrong.

What matters most perhaps, is the *continuation* of the 'Happy Surprise' and *imploded sensation into your sung notes*. From this position, clean, bright sound will grow.

Now, with all these ingredients take *one of your vowels*, gently within your open position and sing this sound for some time, making space and feeling 'retraction' around it: 'inhalare la voce'; it will become even clearer, more *ringing* and your breath will last longer than usual.

Our muscles thrive on the right kind of work and effort. The larynx is a miracle of compact mechanism — floating rather than fixed; lubricated by glands within. Water is needed frequently by singers: it is good to see them carrying supplies wherever they go.

FREEDOM AND AGILITY

WE HAVE IDENTIFIED the breath-take and the start, as the 'centre', the 'core' of our sound. We can, equally, allow our attention to move away much of the time — rather like free-wheeling on a bicycle. This kind of freedom is part of the skill or knack of singing light, fast, agile coloratura passages. It was during the time of the great Bel Canto teaching that the larynx was noted as being capable of something quite special and different — ideal for agile singing.

Still remembering our buoyant stance; alert countenance and spacey open throat we can tackle a melisma — a fast-moving passage of notes that we have *already learned* in our minds — by allowing our voice-box to bounce, or gently oscillate in a manner quite unlike the usual steady, well-behaved position which is suitable for *all* other types of singing. The voice-box takes over with excellent results: a singer then finds his or her *own* best tempo of rapidity. This can determine, with a little give and take, the tempo of a performance.

Singers who read this may feel that they achieve and enjoy the florid type of singing *by instinct*, and indeed some do, as with other aspects of technique. But they also 'lose' the knack every now and again and resort to pushing, perhaps during descending passages where it is easy to slacken the entire system inadvertently. The technique I am trying to describe, once *felt*, lifts the burden of chance and connects fearsome-seeming passages into something nearer a joy-ride. The same method applies to the trill.

The coloratura style reached its peak with Donizetti, Rossini and Bellini. The amazing role of Semiramide was written by Rossini for his wife. These composers understood the voice so well that they balanced the florid passages with spring-board moments when the voice can gather itself together in a *vibrazione* (as will be described later), which does, in fact, constitute the best possible preparation of the mechanism for florid singing.

Joan Sutherland is a great example of a singer who did not develop coloratura singing until she had sung for years in a heavier style — even in Wagner. They say that her husband heard her singing florid passages in the bath! He began to help her develop this technique, and the result has been sensational. As well as her amazing fluency and athleticism, she has also learnt to vary the dynamic and colour of the florid passages with uncanny power. In fact, as she and many others today demonstrate, the skill of this facet of singing is coming back most impressively.

Exercises for Agility

Exercises for agility need your trust in the remarkable capability of your own larynx to do something quite novel and unlike its behaviour at any other time. This is an oscillation of the entire voice-box when you give it 'permission' to do so. *But*, it can only respond freely to your wishes if you *already know the notes of the passage in question*.

Learn the notes carefully (and slowly) with a very light sound. Maintain as usual your tall, proud stance, your widely-opened throat and alert countenance. The climate will then be right for this oscillation to happen freely and carry the movement of runs, melismas, cadenzas and trills.

As soon as this knack works, the feel is of surprising ease. Do not be anxious about the exact tempo of the rapid notes: every singer varies a little in what is their natural 'running speed'. Do not insist on any particular dynamic, either — allow the sound to be as it comes ... lightish. Later, with repetition, the sound will grow a little and will be available when wanted. Any forcing of the issue produces an unpleasantly spread, wobbly sound, which is far from your real purpose.

The skill of agile singing was deeply entrenched in the Bel Canto system, and the composers of the times made tremendous use of it, encouraging great virtuosity among singers, while the abilities of the voices trained in Bel Canto no doubt inspired composers in return. There are many books of vocal exercises that you can enjoy working from, and there are phrases from Rossini, Donizetti, Bellini, Handel and others. But for those who want to experience the feel more gently, I suggest at first only five, or even three, notes on the vowels 'e' and 'a', or corresponding words such as 'yes' and 'laugh' followed by a longer span over the octave.

Agility

Light, spacey — in a laughing position. Sing an 'a' or 'e', or 'laugh', 'dance' or 'yes'. Move the exercise up and down the scale.

Let the notes ripple ... feel more space over the top!

There are many more elaborate shapes required or desired by the singer as your skills grow — use them as you wish.

In Bel Cantists' times the ability to perform and elaborate coloratura was very competitive: the elaborations were called 'gorgheggi'.

As you practice your agility, feel not only the freedom of this knack but also the freedom of the body, helped by changing your weight as you wish and allowing the arms to rise freely, particularly on a downward run so as to keep the rib cage high and buoyant, just where you are tempted to slacken and let go your support. Phrases from Rossini's operas are ideal for agility practice; you will notice how his phrase shapes constantly ask the voice to anchor at special moments, followed by release into the lightness of the next melisma. To be able to do this, to 'intensify and release', is a vital skill and not as difficult as it sounds.

When you are at ease and aware of what is happening, aware of notes almost bubbling along in your throat, try the same idea with a *trill* of one tone's difference (originally a trill of a major third was exercised). Be content with a clear tone, and relieved that most trills we are asked to perform are of only a semitone.

The Trill

Light, buoyant. Let it bounce *lightly*. Much space at back of throat. An oscillation of the larynx.

Sing this quite simply, until the movement in your throat is rather like a ball bouncing gently . . . which it continues to do independently. Again, use no pressure but instead 'stand back', so to speak, making more space 'behind the voice' to enable the larynx to perform — to oscillate at your comfortable speed. All this goes along with your alerted high resonances.

STUDENT: Oh I get *stuck*! (A pushy sound emerges).

TEACHER: Try again as though you were 'drinking back', behind the sounds, making lots of space and let the oscillation happen.

STUDENT: The more I try the worse it is.

TEACHER: Yes. But *don't* try; your kind of trying is actually pushing. *Let* it happen. Give it a little time, without over-trying. If it doesn't work today, it will tomorrow. It is a new process. Your thoughts haven't quite met up with the required muscles. It is rather as though you were asked to waggle your little toe: you could not obey instantly, but would have to think it through and feel it out. Once you have got hold of this agility, nothing will stop you doing it around the house.

STUDENT: I hope so! In the meantime, I had better do it as I used to and gradually incorporate the new way.

TEACHER: That sounds sensible.

STUDENT: I find my runs get blurred as they descend.

TEACHER: Yes, indeed. Singers constantly let themselves and their support down as the notes come down — an instinct, but we should resist it. Keep, and re-assert your support on descending passages, and retain the alertness of your face. Try allowing your arms to rise freely as notes descent.

STUDENT: What if I can't?

TEACHER: You'll go on as before with a sort of hit and miss — maybe more hits than misses: your muscular memory will

tend to remember the 'hits' not the 'misses', and will build
on this constantly.

Portamento
This is about carrying the sound, binding, legato over
intervals of any and every distance.

'Che non lega, non cantare — who does not bind, does
not sing'.

The Bel Cantists were keen to cherish the purity and
clarity of tones through intervals of whatever distance:
keeping vowels constant — clean — ringing undisturbed.
Portamento was then, and still is, very important. The
simplest exercise for this is one of 'rocking' the voice gently
over intervals: joining, carrying, lightly slurring (which
students often think is a musical sin, and sometimes used in
the wrong place, it is!)

Try this on two vowels that you can link smoothly.

e   a   e   a   e   a   e

While doing this exercise, the feeling is of drinking, suction,
'*trust*' —

Then make other shapes with bigger intervals. Also apply
the idea to exercising awkward intervals in the music you
are studying.

Sometimes crescendo upon one of the higher notes:
implode — purify the sound ... 'retract' ... find the steadi-
ness and quality. Your breath lasts longer!

Portamento exercises were much sung and enjoyed by
Jenny Lind — swinging the intervals at all speeds — sometimes very fast until the 'join' disappears.

VIBRAZIONE — VIBRANCY

THE EXPERIENCE AT the source or onset of the sound has been described as 'the caress of the glottis' and was fundamental to the Bel Canto system. Having worked at finding the start of our sound, we can then work at encouraging the 'core' of all our vowel sounds — at increasing our inner muscular control of these sounds in depth. This is done with two basic exercises, first *vibrazione* (vibrancy), then *messa di voce*.

Vibrazione is a brief moment of total intensity and depth — an instant ingathering of total energy and vitality into the vowel in question, with extra buoyancy of breath support rising in balance; and then, by the nature of it, an instant release. It was indicated constantly by all the great Bel Canto operatic composers who understood the voice as the 'bearer of emotion', and was surely welcomed by singers. Though, after Verdi, it was no longer so clearly indicated, it is still — and will forever be — a part of a fine singer's equipment. The traditional sign for it was the small 'v' above the note, but today there is a vagueness about it: it *could* be marked above the note with < or > or even *nothing*, or Sf for sforzando which is not the same. *Vibrazione* is hard to describe but it is strong in 'feel', and it is the beginning of a joyful adventure into a world of expression — depth and colour — *Messa di Voce* and intensity.

Rightly understood, the use of *vibrazione* is the finest *vocal tonic*. The notion of intensity and then release was understood musically and emotionally by the great composers of the seventeenth, eighteenth and early nineteenth centuries (including Mozart) who explored and celebrated this way of helping the voice in the coloratura style. When you acquire the skill of vibrancy followed by release, the most daunting phrases become not only possible to perform but a delight — and bring such energy in the doing that you will look at runs, melismas, cadenzas and decorative cascades of notes in a new light.

Exercises for Vibrazione or Vibrancy

These exercises need concentration and inner muscular athleticism, and are of the greatest value to any student of singing once fully grown — at the age of around eighteen years or so — and on through the entire singing life.

As I have said, it is a *brief moment* of vocal depth and intensity as we sing into the centre of the vowel, meeting the uprising breath at the vocal cords. Or, more simply: think of making the vowel in question *very important* for an instant; not aggressive, or pushed — more as though you greatly *care* about this sound or word. After a brief moment of vowel intensification the sound *releases itself*, it 'bounces back' like a released spring prepared for the flexibility needed for the following notes.

Try it on the word 'sing' or 'yes', deepening the 'i' or 'e' vowel on any note in your middle octave; note your buoyancy coming up to meet the sound.

If the notion of 'deepening' escapes you at first, think of making the word 'yes' extremely important to you — brief but vital! Anchor into the importance of the vowel.

A student of mine said that the moment of emphasis (or depth) into the vowel felt like jumping onto a trampoline —and the release is the bounce back!

A 'pear-shaped' note on the word 'sing', or on the vowel 'i' on its own. The vowel is your anchor.

or 'e' on its own

or 'a' on its own.

Here is the same idea, but 'on the move', swinging along, syncopated:

On same vowels or words as before, swing this arpeggio, with light first note and then four *vibrazioni*, making a syncopated effect, and lightly down again still *open* throated. Swing your arms; walk, dance to the rhythm.

In the exercise below the longer note carries the *vibra-zione*, which is released at once, enabling you to sing the small notes *very* lightly — as a decoration.

Si	-	i	-	-	ing
Ye	-	e	-	-	es
Lo	-	o	-	-	ong
Da	-	a	-	-	ance

Sing freely. Release the *vibrazione before* the small notes — which will 'sing themselves'. Move this exercise up and down. Your 'support' adjusts itself.

A beginner trying these ideas may push his (her) tummy out, and sink the chest, 'thrusting' the accented note, instead of deepening it.

STUDENT: Is this right?

TEACHER: *No!* The opposite would be right. Try bringing your 'usual' support up to meet the vowel — a smart, quick gesture. Keep the top of you tall, broad, high …

STUDENT: I've got it now: rather a good feeling of strength and control.

For many this is hard to get hold of until all at once it feels easy and right. At that moment you have anchored your thought and your vowel into the expression and the body instantly responds. The vowel leads, it brings the support with it.

Next try a combination of agility with the spring-board notes of *vibrazione*. This gives a 'bouncy' anchor from which the freedom of the running notes takes off. There are

many ways of trying it out, not least by taking phrases from
Rossini (and others): a kind of trampoline effect!

Agility and *Vibrancy*

si — — ing si — — ing
ye — — s ye — — s

When singing on 'yes', place 's' as late as possible, taking the
vibrazione on 'e'. The vowels 'i', 'a', 'e' are useful at the middle
and lower ranges, 'oo' and 'o' at the higher — or use 'moon',
'long' and 'dance'.

MESSA DI VOCE
Expression — Dynamics

THE WORDS 'MESSA di Voce' cover the overall use of expression in all its dynamics and 'colours', all made possible by varying the inner strength of the muscles that we have been exercising, with all resonances available, which together will answer your interpretive wishes.

The most common fault in all singing endeavour is to push the breath when wanting to perform a crescendo — the biggest skill to learn is about the containment of strength where breath and sound meet, enabling the singer to perform a crescendo by means of 'intensity', *not* push.

This can be understood and worked as a direct development from the exercises for *vibrazione*. Its effect is to deepen the core or 'content' of the sound not only for a brief moment, but *continually* during the span of a dynamically arched phrase — a crescendo followed by a decrescendo — until our entire strength is involved in the core of the sound. The physiological explanation of how this is done is difficult but the 'feel' is strong and available to all who wish to try it out and work at the inner athleticism needed.

This gathering of intensity at the core of the sound needs great skill because our inner control must take place over an *extended* period of time during which the dynamic of the phrase is shaped. This needs more extended control than did the last brief moments of depth in the *vibrancy* exercise. It has been likened to the pressure at the nozzle of a garden hose, variable in its resistance to the steady flow of the water: as the nozzle is tightened the same pressure of water goes further, with a more intense jet.

The Bel Canto teachers, I am certain, taught this skill by demonstration and did not attempt to describe it exactly in words. The only printed description I have ever read of *messa di voce*, partly in diagram, is a comparatively recent one by Sir Henry Wood, whose books on singing are not known to many (and are very witty). He was clearly devoted to the Bel Canto method, recognizing its insistence on a controlled vowel line from within — flexible and balanced. 'Right action at the generator', he called it. It was also referred to by Franklyn Kelsey, another teacher with a deep understanding of singers' needs, as 'a continuous vocal gesture, or caress of the glottis, in which the vocal tone is conceived as a unity.'

Messa di voce tends today to be forgotten, or misunderstood. But singers now need to understand it correctly more than ever before, because the demands made on them are so heavy. The pressures are infinitely greater than they were 100 years ago: huge opera houses to fill, huge orchestras to surmount, huge journeys to be undertaken very fast; unremitting schedules, higher acting standards expected, maybe un-vocal music to sing, not to mention all the excitements and hazards of music theatre and its daring and demanding directors.

Without the precious skill of *messa di voce*, and all that it implies, a singer's strength and security falters, particularly over the extremities of the vocal range. Some singers have enough instinct to survive, and do so splendidly; but most begin to push for more loudness. They are generous and know no other way of giving their all. At first this 'pushed' tone may sound 'exciting'. But the cost is great, and gradually there comes a 'waver' in the sound that may develop into worse. And then comes distress, or even panic. The fine edges of the vocal cords could be temporarily roughened, or worse.

I have found over many years, and with many professional singers, a *resistance* to discovering this inner core — a resistance to inner awareness. Is it the time it takes? In fact, I think the resistance is more often to the 'exposure' it requires of a *depth* of expression and feeling. Also, the experience of opening a space in the throat is perhaps akin to the trepidation of laying oneself bare — naked — in order to allow the heart of the sound to ring out. The moment this is achieved, the vocal muscles seem to take over and lead the sound, and trepidation turns at once into control and security: mastery at the centre of our vocal mechanism.

The tendency nowadays is, however, towards 'forward focus', taken to mean a forward direction of tone, concentrating the 'feel' of it in the singer's 'mask', and this 'feel' indeed needs to be strong, but do not let it by-pass the heart of the matter. Singers may be fine artists and may put their emotional strength into notes without *true* centring. The effect can approach hysteria. 'Exciting' maybe, but there is a sense of 'going over the top', disturbing to the listener, and dangerous to the singer. Those who can, and do, find the heart of their sound are rewarded by a great freedom and the discovery that the flow and 'carry' of the tone is *just as 'forward'*, and, in addition, picks up resonance and colour from the availability of more space within. Their sound has a ring and vitality to it that carries everywhere.

Franklin Kelsey wrote in his book, *The Foundations of Singing*,

> In singing, every variation of tone-intensity or colour requires a specific shaping of the pharynx as resonator for the laryngeal tone.

Eminent singers of the past stressed the importance of opening up the pharynx. They knew that fine vocal quality depends on its configurations. Tito Schipa said that an egg could be put behind his tongue into his gullet while he was singing. Lilli Lehmann, when she sang, had the sensation that her tone stood on a column of air or on a fountain in her throat. Francesco Lamperti, the famous teacher of the last century, described the sensation of an enlarged pharynx accompanying fine voice-production by saying that the singer should imagine that he was drinking a glass of wine or continuing to breathe in while singing. Caruso is reported to have said that he got the sensation that his tone did not travel forwards through the mouth but backwards.

Apart from technical exercises which follow, and which pin-point and develop pharyngeal extension, *commitment to the text* and musicianly singing also help the technique enormously. The core of the sound can also be found through *sincerity* — the direction of the emotion expressed through the most meaningful words. Yes. Interpretation and technique can and *do* marry and go along together with enhanced purpose. Our instinct overrides our conscious technical craft.

The following exercises for *messa di voce* need much control and inner effort, which is healthy. Don't allow them to get tedious and don't get tight; if you do, walk around, let go, make funny faces, let your tongue move around in your mouth — open up your throat and 'retract' making sure you are breathing silently (the 'Happy Surprise' position). The singing 'organ' only exists when functioning fully. If one part fails, the entire stretching and tensing forces are reduced.

Now we will develop the feeling we've found in the *vibrazione* exercises into those for the *messa di voce*. Here the increase in weight, sonority and intensity is *steady* and

shaped to form a crescendo — of whatever length you plan
— followed by a decrescendo which *still* needs all your
inner strength. Indeed, mysteriously, it seems to need even
more strength and control. Later, with experience, you will
sense the vowel tones controlling your expenditure of
breath, which will go much farther than expected!

Try first on one note:

i - i - i - i - i - i — *or*
Si - i - i - i - i - ing

also triad plus one

and then on this shape:

Si - i - i - i - ing   •Ye - e - e - e - es

Sing also on 'long', 'moon' and 'dance'. Keep vowels clean not
breathy or muddy.

STUDENT: This is very hard work!

TEACHER: So it is! Engaging all your inner strength; hard to
   explain until you actually *do* it. When correctly done, the
   athletic action also *generates* strength, as I am sure you
   will notice soon. The exercises need not be too slow — use
   a tempo that you can support well.

STUDENT: I seem to be running into trouble? Catarrh or
   something?

TEACHER: Yes. It's the tickle of catarrh. The intense inner vibration of the larynx area as we do the *vibrazione* and *messa di voce* stirs up and dislodges bits of catarrh (phlegm), if any is lurking — which there usually is with most of us in our unsunny climes. It only gets thoroughly stirred up when we begin to 'sing in depth'. It is *good* to move it in this way. In fact the *vibrancy* exercise is excellent for clearing the voice before a performance, and, indeed, to get going each day. Find the notes nearest or *at* the tickling point and work at *vibrancy* (or briefly deepened vowels) right *into the tickle*. This can only do good, and takes merely a minute or two to do.

STUDENT: (later on) I've grown to like this exercise, and *rely* on it to loosen catarrh, and to 'get myself together'.

Here is a more advanced exercise for *messa di voce*, using Italian words. The first note is a light spring-board note. Feel the octave jump *before* you get there with throat wide open, almost like drinking. Use portamento.

I have used this S shape. It is meaningful for me.

S for 'Suction': or the feeling of 'imploding' — the upper curve of the S stands for the Space at the open pharynx — the lower curve stands for the shape of the braced collarbone area.

Ma	–	ri	–	i	–	i	–	i	–	i	–	a	*(Maria)*
Ve	–	de	–	e	–	e	–	e	–	e	–	re	*(Vedere)*
For	–	tu	–	u	–	u	–	u	–	u	–	na	*(Fortuna)*
Ta	–	do	–	o	–	o	–	o	–	o	–	ro	*(Tadoro)*
A	–	ma	–	a	–	a	–	a	–	a	–	to	*(Amato)*

Change the vowel and Italian word *in this order* as you move higher — the S sign stands for 'suction' at the open throat between intervals.

The Great Scale — gathering of intensity — choose one of five vowels. The 'i' and 'e' work best for the middle range.

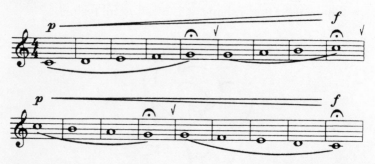

A steady build of depth and intensity at a tempo you and your support can well manage. Deepen into the centre of the vowel as far as you can, buoyantly supported by the lower tummy, groin and tail muscles. The dynamics can be reversed. Your high resonance ring must be with you.

Let this downward scale run lightly; and as it ascends feel
the natural upsurge of support from lower tummy and up
through the body; assert this again on each of the three last
notes. Sing the scale freely.

Sometimes you may feel that you need to draw more
support from your body than is already available — if so,
find it in any of the areas that 'suit you': the base of the
tummy, groin muscles; the tuck-in of the tail muscles which
gives an instant boost of power — the braced collar-bone
area — *the lower back muscles*. They all connect.

RESONANCE

RESONANCE IS THE result of an initial sound. Like many other words we use in connection with singing, it suggests different things to different people. The 'ring'? The 'carry' of the sound? The 'buzz'? The colour? Resonance in fact depends on every singer's personal bone structure — of the head, neck and chest, and particularly across the breast-bone, especially when well 'braced'. Indeed, the entire torso carries resonance. Variations of resonance are infinite: they are also 'catching', in the sense of infecting, from one area to another. This surely accounts for the endless personal timbres and varieties of voices.

An area of resonance that we clearly need all the time and which we can cultivate is the *highest available level* that we can find: the one which is felt across our cheeks, eyes and forehead. I have heard the feel described as a 'saddle' across the bridge of the nose. We can bring this area alive with a certain kind of humming: a feel of 'buzz' if we can find it. We can wriggle the tops of our faces ... widen the nostrils as though smelling something. The Italians worked at this 'smelling up' notion until awareness reached high into the forehead — the *'imposto'*. If it all seems very elusive, don't chase the sensations too keenly. One can encourage things with imagination — even fantasy. Sometimes, however, a sensation fades with familiarity. Don't despair: it may have made its impact and become a part of our precious *muscular memory* which feeds our progress steadily, enabling us to be always in charge.

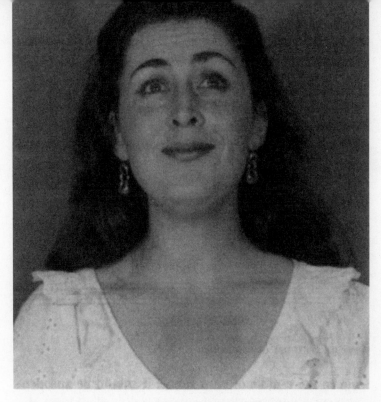

STUDENT: I can feel a bit of a 'buzz' across my cheeks and eyes and forehead — not much — but enough to know my higher resonances are awake. I try to 'switch on' from this area when I need to.

TEACHER: Good. This is the position for your 'open hum' exercises: lips loosely closed, and *open* at the back of the throat. Feel wide open nostrils and a 'smelling up'. Two or three minutes of this at the beginning of your day helps take the 'weight' off the rest of the voice before it is warmed up. We all need to feel sensitive to this part of our sound.

You can even practice this on public transport! The sound is tiny — the exercise is more about 'feel'.

Exercises for Resonance
I have described briefly how resonance enhances our sound
and how we can encourage one particular area, the *highest*
level of resonance. This is the area across the cheeks, eyes
and forehead where we need to be particularly alive and
alert.

The exercises for doing this can be invented by you: I
suggest only a simple hum of three notes:

The Open-Throated Hum

Move up by tones or semitones

Begin in the middle of your range; it should be an open-
throated hum. Your lips should be lightly closed and the
back of your throat *open* — that same openness that you
find as you take every breath. Now 'switch on' the sound at
the level of the top of your cheeks and eyes, as if by-passing
the larynx. Imagine you have a separate switch at this area:
be content with a tiny sound, and, hopefully, a certain high
feeling of 'buzz'; take a little fresh breath after every five
notes, relaxing completely in between them. Each time sniff
or 'smell up' the hum with wide nostrils; as you move high
you *may* get a little thrown at the 'change' of register (the
passaggio) between approximately c' and f' (for sopranos),
but with manoeuvring you may take your hum *very* high,
and into a *falsetto* as high as a bat's squeak. You are airing
the top rooms in your 'vocal house'.

This exercise is a great 'starter', gentle, but telling. The feel,
or sensation, is not spectacular, and in fact there may be very

little, but please do it all the same. Stop only if there is involvement or strain at the throat. The hum should have its own independence. If there is 'involvement' — a kind of 'catch' — with the throat, please *stop*, shake yourself free, and start again directing the sound to the *imposto* (the top of the 'smelling-tube') mid-forehead.

When you have been as high as you wish, take the three notes down an octave and work the same shape downwards, still keeping the idea of high resonance. Working in this way also helps any catarrh that may be bothering you in the sinus area. The attempt to draw — sniff — smell up, moves the liquid or phlegm to some extent. You may feel it moving down at the back of the throat (pharynx) which gives relief.

STUDENT: I find this difficult and fiddly, and I do get my throat involved.

TEACHER: If it 'catches' your throat, STOP, relax, think about something else, then try again. At first it may be tedious, but every singer I have worked with becomes devoted to this exercise. You can then proceed without over-doing things because you are aware of a ring in the sound coming from this high level of resonance.

In contrast to this gentle hum, try some stronger 'ugly' hums on ngi — nge — nga — really nasal — *un*pitched — high and low anywhere, like a game — yet supported always. Try also, if you wish, 'furious' sounds or '*miaouw*' like an angry cat! Then a sweet '*mioouw*' like a contented cat. Wriggle the muscles across the top of your face — nostrils — cheeks to ears . . . now back to those strong ngi — nga sounds, followed at once with vibrant open-throated, centred 'i', 'e', or 'a' (and later, 'oo' and 'o') on three notes — ngi . . . etc.

The ring of your sound will astonish you.

Finally, try out a wonderfully helpful kind of 'hum' combined with other 'noises' sounding rather like a SIREN.

I learnt this from Joe Estill during her teaching of 'Voice-Craft' and believe it has spread like wild-fire amongst my colleagues and their students.

Start on an 'ng' at any pitch — mouth open easily having taken breath, allow sound to 'siren' up and down as low and as high as it likes — gradually as high as a bat and as lightly as you like, or whatever dynamic, and as low as a growl — and high at the top of your sound try a very light (imploded) laugh — or a light whine … the siren can have endless personal variations. Your inner machinery is exercising, stretching, enjoying itself — always connected with 'support'.

Some experts say that the cavities in the sinus area are not part of the resonating system — yet I do find that all singers can feel something to the contrary. Awareness of sound in this area is reassuring and so much alive that at times it becomes the 'steering wheel of our car'. Our varied bony structure vibrates and is surely part of the *individual personality* of our sound — rather as our physical appearance varies. By the way, when singers are very alert in this area across the cheeks and eyes they always look their best!

Related to all this, I have to add a memory when, as a student, I was told that the great singer and teacher Lillie Lehman said, 'I hang the muscles of my face over my ears'. I giggled at this: I now find it a helpful thought!

'COVERING THE SOUND' AND REGISTERS

'To cover or not to cover?' is a question that concerns singers and their teachers a great deal. It is a term that is understood and misunderstood freely.

The term refers to a deliberate alteration or modification of the vowel shape which is thought to be useful or even essential, as the voice moves through its changes of register, particularly the higher of these two areas, between c" and f" for women, and an octave lower for men. Over these areas the laryngeal muscles rearrange themselves into a slightly different position so as to give the vocal cords and the singer a further span of notes.

A register has been defined as that part of the vocal compass which betrays no necessary change of tone quality — without experience you could be excused for thinking that the notes at the upper change are the top or end of your vocal range because negotiating around these notes can be so awkward. Yet, as soon as we find how to open the door we have freedom of many more notes — with care and time this 'change' can become a smooth, well-oiled gear change — no longer a problem area.

The singer feels this 'shift' as he gets nearer to, and into, this area: there is a tension which each of us meets and feels a little differently — more or less acutely. The student is uneasy, wondering if his controls have somehow slipped.

He (or she) may at first take evasive action by 'side-stepping' into a 'heady' sound, continuing through this area and beyond but with another voice, allowing the support to sag, and only finding his or her full sound again on higher notes, and top-heavily.

We all have to learn to meet this situation *with the intention of securing one continuous expressive and flexible line*. I do believe that there is a safe and correct plan of campaign as we move towards, into and onwards through these areas. It is to consolidate the all-over position you already have in the middle voice: your supported breath pressure, your spacey, resiliently open back of the throat, and your alert upper facial muscles.

Within this frame, feel the 'centre' of your vowels, remain true to them, and concentrate on their continuing intensity within your alignment of energy. This control needs great concentration in muscle and thought. It is experienced as the singer's same *unaltered position*, yet it 'costs dearer' in these areas. When you can achieve this, it will have the effect of darkening, rounding and intensifying the vowels, which is Nature's way of looking after the acoustic through the 'choice' of resonators.

If, however, you deliberately cover, or organize an actual change of throat, mouth and stance, another kind of sound will take over. There will be an 'off-beam' effect as though dipping the headlights of a car, a loss of your personal sound quality. The ring of the sound is temporarily diverted and so is your true alignment of energy.

If you listen to your favourite singers you will hear different ways of meeting this situation. This is the tenor's particularly exposed area: Caruso did not, I think, contrive any 'cover' but retained the ringing centre of his sound which we can hear even on the old records. Nor does Pavarotti 'cover', though he describes what extreme care he needs to take over the *passaggio*. He feels, he says, as though moving through an hour-glass, which I take to refer to the feeling of precision and intensity as the vowel 'narrows' before blossoming into resonant fullness above the *passaggio*. Every singer will have a different and personal description of the process.

Covering or approximating vowel sounds for *interpretative* reasons is a different matter. This can be effected instantly by our own imaginative wish in every part of the vocal range — as quickly as thought itself. It does not involve a change in the basic vowel position or stance, just a tiny adjustment in resonance shapes, which happens naturally and acoustically.

All singers will have different physical feelings as they explore and make friends with this question of covering or not covering at the crucial areas of the range. Finally, the sensations may fade with familiarity, at which point the muscular memory has safely taken over.

Perhaps because of its inbuilt tensions, this area of the voice is often required to carry the greatest emotional expression, and some skilful composers have made particular use of this quality, notably Benjamin Britten, Verdi and many of the Italian *verismo* composers.

Please be *glad* to accept a strenuous committed attitude that will enable you to *intensify the vowel utterance* as I have already described.

Courage!

The lower 'change' in vocal range is roughly one octave below the area just described. Again we may feel uneasy and our sound seem slack and weak; we may be tempted to try to 'change gear' in some way, hoping to find a more substantial tone.

As before, please try to be faithful to your alert and supported position: bodily, vocally and facially. Make no special movements, only be sure that your throat is still

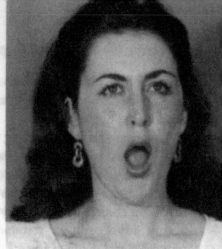

STUDENT: What I am doing now with my expression seems to make for darkening my tone, and I hear a big sound.

TEACHER: It may sound big to your inner listening but the sound is imprisoned and the listeners are not getting any benefit from it and your larynx is pushed down.

STUDENT: You don't seem to like what I am doing?

TEACHER: No, I don't, because you are diminishing your tone, not adding to the whole: in fact it is a 'cover'. You are pulling down the flesh of your cheeks and top lip, and pressing your chin in, all of which cuts off some of your brilliance.

Darker tones can be beautiful and 'noble'. There should always be a mixture of bright and dark, varying in emphasis. Much of this can be found through your mind wishing it so, which magically affects the resonating cavities in subtle ways, together with your braced breast-bone area which carries warm resonance and a comfortably lowish position of the larynx.

STUDENT: Can I find all this and still keep my usual alert expression and open throat?

TEACHER: Indeed you can: in fact I believe you cannot find the colours you want without your alert expression and all that goes with it.

resiliently open. You will soon find that these notes will lead you down, sometimes to surprising depths which relate to the pitch of your speaking voice. Take all this in your stride — enjoy and explore a variety of colours, available here, which carry extra resonance from the chest area. Try giving more or less weight, *but* never allow the sound to become blatant, or pushed uncomfortably into the middle voice. Pushing the chest voice too high can be a real strain and can unbalance your natural sound — and complicate your singing life. The 'pushing' must not be confused with the careful 'belting' already mentioned.

YOUR DAILY VOCAL LIMBERING

IT IS CLEAR that some limbering is necessary most days of our singing life, and, of course, *strictly* on the day of a performance, according to your needs, with the exercises divided into short spells. The voice and its muscular memory like to be reminded of their main functions. By exercising parts of the whole system, singling them out for special attention, the *totality* is then freely available for whatever you require at the time. You are free to make all manner of your own exercises, follow books of vocalise or use bits of your repertoire (carefully). But I do believe that the essentials must be *clear to you as you work*.

In my experience we are all difficult in our relationship with our own voices, as though the voice were 'another person', deeply connected in an emotional love-hate relationship with ourselves: 'How are you, how's the voice?' you hear yourself asked — and you will give two answers!

This may account for our contrary feelings about the process of limbering — opening up and revealing all even to ourselves! It is worth the struggle so that you may feel in good shape to face the world.

Also, I have to add, that students are lazy about the details and *corners* of practice and often bring back the same problems unworked on, which is very wasteful of their time and money — I was no different!

We need to make friends with each type of exercise and so understand why we are doing it and sense the benefits — later on, when you feel familiar with it all, the exercises can be 'condensed' so that you can warm up in a shorter time, if need be.

Vary the order of these exercises according to your needs on each particular day. But never start with the *messa di voce*, because that is the most demanding of all. Rather start with the hum, the start-of-the-note or the agility exercises.

Many singers, at various stages, *avoid* regular limbering of an organized kind, and prefer to make haphazard sounds. Is it because we none of us like putting ourselves on the spot for inspection, even for our *own* inspection? We also cling to the hope that it should and can all happen instinctively — which indeed it can, when all is set fair and right, and particularly for those singers from Mediterranean climes. Again, we may feel so sensitive about this instrument of ours, so deeply important to us, that we cannot face up to disappointing moments. I clearly remember holding back practice for this reason; and similarly, if I were lucky in finding a sound I had been seeking, I would not dare to try it for a second time in case it had disappeared! Yet, taking all of this into account, it is still unwise to avoid organized limbering, however brief.

Exercising is all about alerting your thoughts and muscles — about energising all the many little muscles inside your throat which will draw in the larger muscles of the body and together free the action of the true vocal folds as athletically as possible and encouraging appropriate resonance.

Experienced singers will have their own slant on limbering, yet may wish to pluck a few from this book. With care we can feel 'sung-in' in ten or fifteen minutes — ideally it is best to work for further short periods with other activities between.

If you are the teacher, the ideas within these exercises can be made more fun or playful for your beginners and for children. You will enjoy thinking them out in a variety of ways.

Perhaps most important of all: by re-thinking and re-feeling these skills we are establishing our *muscular memories*. Faulty singing needs no repetition, but if a singer has had a troubled history and now has found the *correct way*, the muscular memory needs a *great deal* of reassurance and guidance — as if leading a child by the hand. The muscular memory needs the *repetition* that will establish a new good habit. Treat your muscular memory with the greatest respect ... consideration ... friendship. 'Knowing' with your *mind* is not enough.

VOWELS AND CONSONANTS

THE FIVE MAIN Italian open vowels are ideal for the singers' training and for centering your sound. From these it is no problem to adapt into other vowels in any language or dialect. I have not managed to learn International phonetics, but I believe that young singers would be wise to do so.

Here are ten English sounds which include five vowels exactly similar to the open Italian sounds:

a	as in	sun	or in	Italian	amato
e	as in	yes	or in	Italian	vedere
i	as in	sing	or in	Italian	Maria
o	as in	not	or in	Italian	tadoro
oo	as in	moon	or in	Italian	fortuna

and here are the others:

ah	as in	father
er (or ur)	as in	mirth
oh	as in	hope
aw	as in	lawn
u	as in	look
ee	as in	feel

We have briefly discussed vowels: their starting place, their centre, the feel of them as an anchor when needed (which we can control), and their emotional expression. Now they can become the stream of sound on which the consonants sit lightly. The message of the words is as important as our musical sounds. For *clarity*, it is necessary to *lengthen* the vowels and *shorten* the consonants. The feel of the definition of the consonants should be kept *high*: not at the lips or mouth but around the nostrils, cheeks, eyes and forehead. This area should be *constantly* active. Labouring the words with mouth and lip-shaping is, in my opinion, quite counterproductive. In fact, these unnecessary movements seem to break up the flow of vowel tone and contribute nothing.

The higher the activity in the face, the clearer the message. Tenors, with their particularly high level of resonance, seem to come off best as regards clarity of diction. Our listeners look at the *eyes* of the singer for enlightenment, not at their mouths. I like to think of the message of the words moving from the singer's thoughts and brain, out through the eyes.

The beginning consonants of a word often get thrown away in favour of a clearer vowel: but a final consonant (where appropriate) jolts the listener into an instant understanding of a word he may have missed. Some of the greatest operatic singers are the *least* easy to understand, their superb vowel line taking over their diction. However, a good compromise must be reached. On the highest notes the singer should 'approximate' the vowel sound to the best 'ringing' sound nearest the vowel called for. The listener's own ear will restore the intended vowel. In the final analysis the singer's *wish* to communicate the message, his or her sincere interest in the words being shared with the listener, is the most effective tool of all. If you care for the words, you will also phrase them musically.

There is much controversy about the use of translations. Using the vernacular does not always help the listener. There *is* a level of comprehension, but there is always a disturbing distance of musical identity from each syllable, word or phrase, with a corresponding loss of the word colours and shapes originally intended. Every language, moreover, seems to carry its own particular *level* of resonance and its own timbre. Surely the highest feel of resonance is in French, in which the overall 'ring' of the sound seems near to tears, or the holding back of tears, somewhere between the eyes?

Italian needs a 'sunny aspect', and its constant open bright vowels encourage the ultimate in a spacey open throat. As a result it gives high efficiency of the laryngeal muscles and an involvement of the entire face, head and, indeed, body. Sometimes they 'round off' a vowel but never cover. Very near to this is Spanish. English and German should not lag far behind: the darker vowels and diphthongs must not 'pull down' the energy of our offering. (What I am saying is approximate and not exact or scientific.)

In the vocal expression of whatever a singer is interpreting, it is wonderful to know that sound is influenced by the will and the imagination in so many ways: tiny inflections of thought influence variations of the resonating areas, rather as minute, barely perceptible changes of facial expression indicate nuances of mood that we 'read' almost subconsciously. Today, more is being revealed scientifically about the effects of thought on the voice. There are apparently tiny shifts in shapes within the pharynx and the various interior parts of the larynx which respond to the singer's thought and imagination. For those singers who dare express themselves, the response in sound is *immediate* — so long as their basic vocal system is working in good alignment.

Consonats

It has been said that consonants are 'acoustical noises'. Articulate briskly in advance of the note — feel the consonants nearer the *eyes* than the *mouth*! Your tongue needs to be very active.

Exercises

'Patter' consonants very precisely: lightly — quickly.

Here are some, all belonging to the nursery!

Mama — Papa — Baba — Tata — Dada

Now any and all other consonants as fast, clearly, briskly as you can — but without 'mouthing' ... la ... la ... va ... va ... etc.

Try whispering words (from your songs) with a finger between side teeth, and feel where consonants are made, *not* interfering with vowel articulation.

If you have no problems with consonants, then all you need is your strong interest in the text which will guide you.

Tongue twisters are helpful — collect a few!

Here is one: 'I want a proper cup of coffee in a proper copper coffee pot'

Say it fast!

Be aware of where consonants are formed, BUT no mouthing:

Lips:	M B P F V W
Tip of tongue:	L N T R D
Back of tongue and jaw:	G K J CH SH Y
Sound 'interrupters':	S P K T

THE WISH TO SING

I HAVE LEARNED my trade as a voice teacher partly through my own difficulties, described elsewhere, and also from my students, including amateur singers, whose longing to use their voices against all odds is astonishing. The huge desire to express something through one's own body can emerge most strongly in teenage years. However modest the singing talent may be, I have always taken the wish to sing very seriously indeed. For I believe *everybody* owes it to themselves to get their voices working correctly and freely. There will then be no regrets and much to be gained.

The wish to sing and open up one's personality means physically *opening up the back of the throat*; literally the gateway to freedom and expression. The involvement of the entire person, voice — body — feelings. The British temperament does not encourage this, nor does the English language with its closed word-endings. Even professional students, who are more extrovert, perhaps, find the true sunny Italian 'a' sound hard to find. It is a sound that cannot be made without *total* back-of-the-mouth and throat opening. It can feel like a physical exposure. The Italian language is, indeed, the great 'opener'. Its characteristic vowel word-endings and their throw-away action give the singer a wonderful 'bounce' — *so* different from English, which tends to clamp our jaws as we finish nearly every word. But this is no excuse to sing English carelessly. When sensitively done the language is beautiful and subtle.

The inability to get the throat open (to retract the false

vocal folds fully) and to animate the face, which so many experience, is hardest for the *very* introverted and/or depressed person. It often happens that one of the first overt signs of depression is a falling-off of the voice, a loss in the timbre of the vowels, and an over-relaxation of the soft palate and the pharynx. Depressed people very often mumble. The voice sinks, and even eating can become a problem because the springy resilient opening of the throat just isn't functioning. The front of the face — the actual countenance — drops, so resonance around the sinuses is suddenly curtained off. This is one way in which a depressed person reacts to the world. The body goes slack and there is no support.

I have been asked to work at singing as a therapy by Jungian analysts who relate healing and creative expression very closely. In the *early* stages of depression the basics of vocal technique, especially the 'happy surprise' breath and the start-of-the-note exercises, are a great lift. The emerging sound can give hope and confidence. I used to say, rather sweepingly, that singing and depression could *not* go together. But I have learned now not to expect too much when a person's depression is deeply entrenched. In fact, trying too hard might be an irritant and a further worry.

I have also tried to help the ailing elderly. If they can make a 'happy surprise' position and so pick up the uvula and soft palate this can remedy their very common coughing and choking over food and drink which is often the result more of mild depression than of *anno domini*. This over-relaxed position of the uvula which some, not only the elderly, fall into while sleeping is, incidentally, one of the main causes of snoring.

I believe the wish to sing is intimately bound up with the desire we all have to know and express ourselves. 'Are you your voice?' I ask, applying the question both to speech and singing. Ideally, we would all answer 'yes'. But it is not so easy. There are all sorts of pressures on us to produce certain kinds of sounds. Our speech is almost as much a part of our social uniform as the clothes we choose. The growth of recording has put a similar pressure on singers, who often try to sound like the stars they hear on records, rather than search for their own sound.

Youngsters should stay with their *own sound* and not imitate — with or without singing lessons try not to make a contrived sound.

Your muscles will gradually strengthen, especially with the help of a good teacher. Above all, youngsters and their elders should try and emerge from the deadpan utterance we hear around us, which can actually harm you — and bore others! Instead try and enjoy the flexibility of your voice in speaking as well as singing. Let your own personality emerge: you will feel happier.

TENSION IN PERFORMANCE

WHATEVER OUR INSTRUMENT or form of expression we all feel uneasy when confronted by even the notion of *tension/strain/nerves*. It can choke and well-nigh cripple us, yet when unlocked, it can be an electric charge for us to harness and use to our great advantage.

We singers may understandably feel that we come off badly because we are our entire instrument for good or ill, and so totally vulnerable. At our vocal centre is our larynx — small, intricate, invisible, almost unfeelable, yet as magical as the micro-chip. We ourselves, our bodies, are the scaffolding around this little wonder and we need to give all our attention, our athletic poise and strength, our minds and feelings to set it working freely. Its response to our thought is lightning quick. Yet our general health and our moods vary endlessly: we can be exalted, we can feel shattered, and so many gradations between. In spite of all this, somehow we can, and do, keep our voices surprisingly steady.

I want to explore some positive ways of building up our 'fortress' of performing strength; but, first, I must indulge in some painful personal memories. As I've said, I confess to having been a singer in constant technical difficulty — only resolved later in life. Yet I had a very strong wish to meet the public and communicate. So there was always conflict and insecurity.

Working on a programme was exciting and I was always full of hope, even joy — interspersed with panic. As time went on, panic became dominant. Then, on the day of the performance, something near paralysis set in, as though I was suspended in time and space, somehow immobilized, with no concentration for anything at all. All seemed unreal. 'Am I ill? Will I be sick? I am desperately tired and heavy as lead. Why do I try to sing? This is not the profession for me! Never again! . . . My throat has seized up . . . there is a thick fog of catarrh . . . I am voiceless! . . . '

Then, a push on to the platform or stage and there was, sometimes, an amazing magic — an instant flow of concentrated energy, a conversion into another coinage! Where had it come from? But the nightmare was too high a price to pay.

Such pre-performance pains are, of course, very variable, and they do, to some extent, depend on how well, or otherwise, we know our job. Our fundamental security must come from knowing our craft, so that our technique is our 'friend' and can never wholly let us down. Not surprisingly, therefore, it is a fact that the 'instinctive' or 'natural' performers often suffer worst, and are most vulnerable to pre-performance tension.

I know of a tenor of world stature (who gave me some singing lessons years ago) who was frozen with nerves before each performance even at the height of his career. His voice sounded wholly secure, but he was completely innocent of its workings — and of the workings of the music — and his subconscious may well have been saying: If my memory slips, I am lost. He had never learnt musical notation, relying totally on a quick ear and slogging away with stalwart repetiteurs. Out there on his own, both voice and music relied on instinct alone — terrifying.

I remember, too, Kathleen Ferrier, during her wonderful yet so short career, feeling very differently before a performance: 'Like a racehorse rarin' to go,' as described by her pianist, Gerald Moore. Not long ago I read some lines by Luciano Pavarotti describing in his own way how he feels when the overture begins: 'The curtain rises, I know from many past performances that I am blessed with a quality that helps me, when the moment is upon me, to lose these paralysing nerves; it is like self-hypnosis, and is hard to explain.'

Some less experienced singers sometimes feel *too relaxed* before a performance, and, later, when in action, can be overtaken by tension and nerves in mid-stream. This is really hard to combat and much more alarming. So be glad if you are one of those whose nerves and nervous energy are available at the 'proper time'. Because 'nerves' can be *positive* and can *contribute* to our performance and convert into adrenalin and energy.

A colleague, Carola Grindea, writes that tension is a healthy phenomenon and is indeed an immense gift for which we must be grateful. I agree. Channelled correctly, tension is nothing but that very same energy we need to vitalize and maintain our vocal mechanism. The more familiar we are with the way that this mechanism works for us, the more we can make *positive* use of tension.

So the most important approach to security in performance is to work on your own physical awareness and well-being by getting on good terms with your vocal technique. The technique that I so greatly believe in, which is described in this book, is ideal for steadying the singer in times of stress. Whichever area of the system we can sense at a particular moment we can use to bring the whole system into alignment. If it suits the moment to feel and emphasize the space behind and around the voice-box then 'vowel centering' can become the focus for our energy; or we can go deeper into certain vowels, when 'spaciness' will improve; or if we want to concentrate on high resonance,

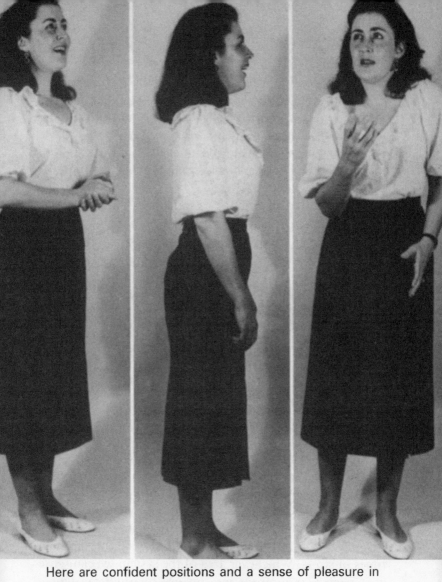

Here are confident positions and a sense of pleasure in 'being there' and sharing a performance — arms and hands must feel that they belong to you, not feeling or looking stiff. They must not compensate dramatically for what you may feel too 'choked' to give with your voice. See our singer happy, but also under stress in the third photograph.

then its special alertness will also open up pharyngeal spaces — the one thought helping the other. Because this technique, like nature itself, is a totality, and can encompass every aspect of the demands made on a singer, those who are familiar with it find that they have 'something to hold on to' — a guide to sensations which are always available.

Auditions

As a teacher I am constantly preparing singers for another, and yet another audition — a necessary and rather painful part of marketing in our profession. Do not be tempted, I say to them, to offer songs or arias which are beyond your own comfort and grasp at this *particular* time. Our development into the repertoire is always on the move and fluid, and there is always time ahead for more ambitious offerings. Bear to be on the conservative side, and not over-daring.

I also point out that each audition is a rehearsal for the next audition. After the preparatory work is done, I still like to see the singers, if possible, on their way to the actual event. This helps to get the voice limbered up and the concentration together, underlining points that seem needed and, hopefully, ensuring a good, buoyant and happy attitude.

Now, although the singer leaves me in excellent fettle, I never know what *actually transpires* during the moment of truth an hour or two later. There may be — and often is — a chemical change. Some singers gather strength; but some are diminished and do less than their best for many circumstantial and psychological reasons, which is distressing, and a puzzle difficult to solve.

For some singers 'delivering' in this arbitrary way feels like a kind of display or prostitution. Some feel it is simply unreal and that communication doesn't work in this kind of cattle market, and they cannot snap out of a negative attitude. Vocal energy suddenly flags. Others have more 'punch', which helps a lot. Having been on both sides of auditions for very many years, the jury knows it is a hard test and takes your response into consideration as they assess the performance.

Much consideration should go into the choice of offering. It may have to be a set piece, but usually what is wanted as a *first* choice is a song or aria that *suits the singer really well*. This will be something in which you are honestly safe and happy and able to show some of your best skills — something belonging to positive and recent work. Very long-time old favourites can unconsciously pull you back into muscular memories that are less impressive than your present strengths. The second piece is usually your auditioner's choice; but if it is yours, make it a good contrast. Foreign languages may be required, but, above all, when singing in your *own* language, let it be clear and eloquent: *believe* in the words and music and strive to *share* them with these 'judges', even if their eyes are down and their hands scribbling comments. Show that you *care* for their interest. Reach out and *draw them to you*.

About dress: men should wear easy clothes, but also tidy! Probably it is best not to wear flashy colours. The neck area must be easy. some polo-neck garments are rather strangulating or inhibiting. Women may choose a long skirt — which is wise on a high stage — 'long lines' are better than wide, chunky clothes. Whatever your figure, let the neck area be free, and the shoulders a little squarish, so that there is not a stoopy look. Waists should not be *too* tight, and colours not blinding. Make-up should be rather stronger than for every day — eyes emphasized but not eyebrows, which if over-darkened can make you look clownish. Hair off your eyes ensure no shadow. (Beware of overhead lighting, and stand a little up-stage of it if possible.) Your eyes are your visible communicators for your listeners' close attention.

'The eyes are the mirror of the voice' said Lampereti (one of the Bel Cantists).

If you wear glasses and feel bereft without them, then wear them. But they do tend to separate you from your listeners a little. If you take them off and do not need to read music, your listeners may become a blurr — not a disadvantage! — and should not lessen your interest in them. The alternative is contact lenses, if you are comfortable with them.

Don't eat just before an audition, because your support muscles will be battling with your digestion and neither will win. But you must not arrive hungary. Though if you *do* get caught with a 'sinking feeling' glucose tablets will buoy up your energy quickly — albeit briefly. Carry water with you.

Auditions are unavoidable for *very* many years. Rightly or wrongly they are taken to be the only valid guide to a singer's performance: sound, style, personality, looks, charms, drawbacks ... You are judged more decisively at an audition than if you are seen somewhere in performance.

Somehow or other, *try* and take auditions naturally in your stride. The situation *can* be made to be positive — and, in any case, there is no other way of selling vocal goods.

The strain and excitement of auditioning becomes greater when they are repeated on the way to the Finals of the big National (and International) competitions. The singer has to present different and equally well learnt and digested groups of varied songs and arias and keep up strength and sparkle. The situation certainly pumps in adrenaline, but of course there are hazards — sometimes the more sensitive performers flag a little, and those emboldened by phenomenal techniques blaze away whatever the circumstances. The ideal survivor is the singer with a balance of both!

Word Memory

Some of us feel that word memory is a particular worry that contributes greatly to pre-performance tension. It was for me. Memorizing at night, just before sleep, is a good time because the brain seems to do a lot of storage work during the night, and, by the morning, the words are sorted out.

Another good idea is to write out your words and carry them about with you — enjoy living with them and consider their mood and meaning, allowing your memory to become friendly with the direction of their thought. Have the words of your forthcoming recital programme in a small notebook so that you can absorb them when travelling around, getting deeper into them. Memorizing will tend to work 'by itself' if you can deepen your understanding of those words and their relationship with the vocal line.

Pacing: Before the Performance

Your discipline on the day of a performance will affect the kind of tension you experience. Of course circumstances vary greatly, and difficult journeys may be necessary. But as nearly as possible try and follow a plan: the morning of an evening concert may be for rehearsal, limbering, travelling. But ideally afternoons must be *free* — or, at least, free for three or four hours before the performance. These hours must be *private*, devoted to one thing only: rest. Rest flat out, a on a bed if possible, or if not a bed, then a surface that is horizontal, warm and comfortable. Sleep if you can. Do not fear that after the sleep your voice will be over-relaxed. You can get it together again, for certain, with a hot drink and five or ten minutes' careful limbering. If sleep will not come to you, relax, however strange and 'suspended in time' you may feel.

Do not socialize during the hours leading up to a performance. It is tempting to do so sometimes. The comfort and distraction of friendly conversation may take the edge off your nerves, but I fear it also takes the edge off your nervous energy, which you greatly need. Also, try to avoid a communal dressing-room that may be full of other people's talk, mostly about themselves and their tensions. You need to store your energy silently, and then the alchemy will happen: the adrenalin will transform your nervous tension into creative energy for your performance.

After the performance your good 'buzz' and excited feelings will stay 'high' for quite a while. Sharing this time with friends is pleasant and very necessary. To be alone is horrid. Most singers also like to eat at this time. Next morning, you and your vocal machine instinctively say, leave us alone: no muscular efforts for at least a day. Singers are required nowadays to push themselves and their voices much too soon after performance: time, money, pressures ... So *please take care*.

Pacing: The Recital Programme

It is a great joy to plan and juggle with all the possibilities of a recital programme. Sometimes you are required to follow the wishes of the organizers to some extent. Your performing life may be just beginning, singing short mixed groups of songs for charity performance or 'dinners', or you may be planning a half or a whole evening's programme for music clubs up and down the country. And, later, it may be your own début recital, on which you are seriously judged.

I remember finding my wish to explore ever new repertoire overtaking discretion! But of course the same advice as for auditions holds good here: do not be tempted to offer songs that are beyond your comfort and grasp at this particular time. But, within this limitation contrasts of mood and of period are very important. In fact, sharp contrasts can carry an audience a great deal further into new fields than they realize — and can sweep away prejudice unbeknownst. The listener remains alert rather than over-relaxed or sleepy, and this will help you, the singer, since you will not have to divert energy into creating attention, which is something that ought to be built into the programme anyway.

A singer needs to settle into the first song easily —making friends with his own sound and the hall, the pianist and the audience. The audience needs these minutes equally to get acquainted with the singer — his appearance, sound and overall impression. In my view, the audience does not listen deeply until after the first song.

The early Italian songs (*Arie Antiche* of the seventeenth and eighteenth centuries) have been used as 'starters' for generations. There is a lot to be said for keeping to this tradition. There is a vast store of these songs and they are written by composers who understood the voice so deeply that the songs are rightly known as 'vocal massage'. Alternatively, the Elizabethan lutenists' songs —vocally less demanding — also ease one into the voice and into the pleasure of beautiful words. After this kind of start, it used to be 'the thing' to move on chronologically. But I believe one is free to juggle time and style tastefully and with intent.

If you wish to present a song cycle, the best time is either immediately preceding the interval or immediately after the interval, when sometimes we feel good, secure and refreshed. If it is to be a modern cycle, even a first performance, then any critics present will probably wait. But otherwise you risk their fairly frequent disappearance at half time!

Only you yourself can feel where in a programme you can give your 'all' dynamically and emotionally. It could be during the final twenty minutes or it might be at several strategic moments during the one-and-a-half hours (approximately) of actual singing. (Two hours including the interval is a good average recital length.)

Singing in one or two languages, in addition to your own, is usually expected and enjoyed. Try to use your own language before others, so that your listeners know your own understanding of words before any barrier comes between you and them, *however slight*. Most singers are excellent parrots, and learn the *sound* of languages quickly. We do not have to be able to converse in these languages, but we do have to absorb every shade and nuance of meaning of the particular songs we are offering, and to soak up the literary background behind the words.

Some people find it useful to develop a visual picture of the content of their programme. I sometimes used to scribble a plan of the mood and shape and 'colour' of a series of songs so that it began to feel like a familiar journey that I was making, ready to share with my listeners. Certainly, one must try to communicate the *total reality* of each composition. *Nothing* must come between you and your audience: neither technique, nor nerves, fears, self-interest — *nothing*!

Your stamina will grow as you learn to pace the programme in rehearsal. Never allow tension to build up: uncontrolled tension can almost strangulate. Indeed, the working of each song or aria needs to be paced with your thoughts, your voice and your entire alignment of energy. However, if tension should build up, there *are* ways of 'shaking yourself free' again: try to make use of every gap in the vocal line — however brief — to free yourself. When practising on your own, this 'shaking free' can be done almost literally — like shaking out a piece of wet washing. In performance the actuality has to be more of a 'notion' in your thoughts, which can, nevertheless, have an instant effect all through your body. Another instant casting off of tension is a gesture of pretended 'sobbing' without the tears — and of course only if you are NOT seen — a tiny moment of deliberate 'collapse'. Then you can gather your energy once again — free of stress.

Each new breath can be a release, instantly, particularly if every breath is taken with the 'happy surprise' idea in mind. Breaths in mid-stream need be no more than a light topping-up. Learn to come off a phrase a fraction *before* time, rather than be late on the next. Begin an expanding passage lightly, with plenty of high resonance at the ready in your thoughts, and across your eyes and forehead. Then intensify the phrase gradually, as required, by allowing the vowel tone to 'take the lead', *not* by pushing the breath and stiffening. Experience in careful pacing is the answer to reducing tension build-ups, and is worth much thought and care.

A Note on Dancers

Female singers who have first trained as dancers are quite often in trouble. Although blessed with agile arms and legs and slim, mobile bodies, there may be stiffness from the lower stomach muscles up to the top of the chest, retained from deliberately learned *breath-holding* for balance skills when on their toes or *en pointe*.

This somewhat rigid control is at odds with the *resilient*

strength needed by the singer as she *exhales*. The dancer-singer now has to find a support *not* locked by the held breath, but controlled and led by her sound, which can be a tricky task. She must try and separate the feel of the braced breastbone and shoulder area from the buoyant control initiated at the bottom end of the support system: the lower stomach muscles and around the groin and buttocks — familiarizing herself equally with both these areas and encouraging their independence.

VOICE STRAIN AND OTHER HAZARDS ...

HOW DOES STRAIN begin? When do we or our listeners notice it? The worst is that it can escape notice in the young singer for a long time.

Young muscles are so resilient that they recover and are constantly ready for more ill-treatment. There are, however, a number of common pitfalls, of which singers should be aware. Choral singing is one, at the same time as being one of the great musical pleasures.

Partly-trained and, of course, untrained singers too often get carried along in choruses or choirs, carried away by enthusiasm. Conductors, unfortunately, very rarely coax their singers correctly, by limbering and warming up voices gently and knowingly. Most of them do not do it at all.

Britain's choral singing is one of our best national assets. The untrained or partly-trained sound is considered ideal for group singing because of its ability to blend — it is a more sensitive corporate instrument, without the vibrato and ring of the professional soloist. But it is wrong that many young choristers tire and feel strained because they have too little knowledge of their own skills to stand up to demands made amid the sounds around them.

When I was teaching in music college, all my part-time students were choristers in trouble, and all asked for help in this aspect of singing. Sometimes I had, reluctantly, to ask them to withdraw from a choir or chorus for a while. Strain also builds up during the years in music college, quite apart from choral singing. The strain may *not* be obvious, because voices are very 'elastic' at this time of life. But the security of technique is often not sufficient to maintain the ambitious programmes tackled. The content and standard of student performances is very high these days, and often greatly acclaimed. A singing student with strong temperament can be in great danger of pushing the voice, even though what we hear is still impressive.

Strain may arise from faulty and/or unwise singing but voice ailments connected with colds, menstruation, bodily ailments or environmental conditions can exacerbate each other and cause much distress. Voices of students who use contraceptive pills have been known to alter in range. Changes of this nature can be adjusted with medical advice.

Our entire capabilities as professional singers can be shattered between one night, when all seemed very well, and the next morning when there appears to be no voice there. Suddenly, awful choices have to be faced: to struggle on and perform gallantly — unwisely, perhaps badly? Or to cancel, and upset management and audiences, becoming known as 'unreliable'? You can't win in this situation, but what matters in the long run is the health of your own instrument.

So now a few words of homely advice, which most of you know: if the onset of a cold is in the head area only, you may sing well — sometimes especially well — but to do so aggravates the development of the cold towards the throat, and once it is in the throat area there is *danger*.

Do *not* sing while it hurts. This is lunacy although occasionally unavoidable, and can set back recovery by a long way.

Later on, after infection has subsided, you feel well and the pain has gone, but the voice may still *not respond*: the muscles are slack and are taking their proper time to recover their elasticity. An 'over-relaxed' throat must be respected. *Don't worry. Try to wait.*

At these moments, nervous singers may make an appointment with a throat specialist and pay a lot of money for reassurance. Be sparing with such visits!

It has been found by ENT specialists that singers sometimes complain of soreness in the throat and an uneasy feel at the vocal folds the next morning after a late meal, however much enjoyed. It is caused by excessive acidity of the stomach — a *reflux* — so avoid rich foods late at night.

Much strain can be felt by singers who let go of their breath support when not singing but *speaking*. They do this as a matter of habit, especially in 'off-guard' situations such as social gatherings, when driving a car, or when called on to speak lines in a performance or introduce songs from the platform. *Speaking* without support is as damaging as *singing* without support. Even professional singers may spend more of their lives speaking than singing, and, if unsupported, it can cause damage which is reflected in the singing voice. Some of the most dangerous times are during long chats on the phone, in various sloppy sitting or half lying positions. Try to find some kind of alignment wherever you are when speaking as well as when singing, on or off the phone!

Wise singers may well put Vitamin C high among their own home remedies for colds. Drinks that are both soothing and sharp — lemon and honey, for instance — are good, but not too many milky drinks. And don't forget to inhale steam from a jug of boiling water when you have discomfort or congestion in the head, lower throat or lungs. I know singers who travel with steam humidifiers for this purpose. Be careful to stay warm after inhaling steam.

As we all know, singers who travel have to contend with

air conditioning and fierce changes of climate that are very disturbing, not to mention long *flights*. When flying, the main thing to remember is not to become dehydrated (aircraft have about 2 per cent humidity, compared with our average English 30 per cent). Flood yourself with bland liquids before, during and after the flight.

Lastly, about *catarrh* — an endless topic in our singing sessions, and an almost constant annoyance in our climate. Instead of the even lubrication we all need around the voice area, we become dry, and there are granules of catarrh that we call 'frogs'. Don't cough them away roughly. You *can* move them away, for at least a few hours, by using certain *voice* exercises: if the congestion is in the face or 'heady' area then try our particular humming exercises to encourage vibration and movement in this area. If the catarrh is lower down, then do please use the *vibrazione* exercises. Taking a vowel in the middle area of the voice, or exactly at the pitch where the catarrh is disturbing you, and briefly intensifying it two or three times as described in the exercises, will satisfactorily shake off the granules by means of inner vibrancy.

Vocal strain can be felt and revealed by its owner in a number of ways: nervous unease, repeated sore throats and discomfort, all-over tiredness during and after performances, even a sense of panic at times. This may be compounded by the quantity of singing done — though that may not be excessive till later in a career. A teacher may be loath to pull that singer back in his tracks, but also may not know of a 'safety-kit' to offer.

Strain is initially caused by *lack of balance* in the vocal system: the balance of the breath pressure, buoyed by the support muscles, against the correct muscularity at the glottis. The 'start of the note', as I so often repeat in this book — the 'feel' of that start — can best be found by relating instantly to the vowel in question, allowing the vowels and breath to interact. But even if this vowel-centre is not fully understood, singers manage without strain if they have sufficient steady and elastic breath support. This is the attribute *needed constantly*, and which must be gathered afresh not only with every breath, but renewed over and over again in midstream. The technique is hard to learn and hard to teach. But blessed are those who have the instinct for it! The most promising voices have just this: it can be seen in these singers' stance; sensed in their approach, heard in their sound which is never coarse.

Never forget that a degree of technique is needed in speech, as well as in song — in teaching and performing, as well as in daily life. Unsupported speech is as dangerous to the singer as unsupported singing.

As years go by, a singer's equipment jibs at faulty or careless treatment. It becomes less flexible, and listeners can hear a waver in the sound in *excess* of the vibrato without which voices do not ring fully. A waver soon becomes a disturbance, a pulse, and at the same time a rigidity. The sound is unyielding, and soon it can be afflicted by the dreaded *wobble*. This wobble, or judder — a frightening word — is extremely hard to reverse. It *can* be done, but is a heavy task for teacher and singer.

Singers who feel the onset of the wobble tend to use *more* breath pressure than the weary cords can properly take — the cords' edges having become slack or rough, unable to adjust to the singer's wishes and meet the breath with precision.

Finally, the cords are driven into swellings, or thickenings at certain points, and the dreaded 'nodules' may appear. These can sometimes be 'rested' away by *complete silence* over several weeks, or they can be operated upon —

something all singers hope to avoid, though the operation is becoming ever more skilful and successful.

To conclude: singers should notice their own strain sooner than the listener. How to act on the knowledge is crucial; but singers' responses are often haphazard, and, without professional help, frequently useless.

Discerning listeners should be able to recognize strain by noting a pushy, breathy (even hooty) quality, rather than a balanced, likeable tone. Or they may see strain in red necks with outstanding veins, perhaps an unnatural jaw position, and an unhappy strained face and hunched shoulders combined with a poor, 'hollow' or flabby stance. Yet again, the signs may not be obvious for several years. Listeners may simply not enjoy that singer's performance.

Tenors

Perhaps the category of voice that reveals strain most obviously is the tenor. The tenor's high tessitura and placement demands great laryngeal strength and tension, which needs to be very well harnessed. The athleticism needed for his higher notes in full voice is tremendous, and if it is not properly balanced, the voice is gripped into a kind of strain which sounds, and is, alarming.

Many good tenors are shortish of build and have very muscular necks, shoulders and chests — indeed, a similar muscular set-up to the weight-lifter. The latter maintains his strength at a tight-shut glottis (vocal folds) against huge breath pressure. The singer retains his strength with the glottis *slightly* open, as breath pressure turns into sound.

No wonder tenors need to be fit and supremely confident. And no wonder that they have the highest record of nervous temperament and tricky personality. Perhaps this explains, too, the endless jokes about tenors. When working with a tenor, I feel instinctively 'on his side'. He has to keep his inner strength even stronger as the voice moves over the *passaggio*, without relenting for an instant, or he will fall off the tightrope. It is a trial of strength for him (and for his teacher!). A tenor who cannot face this will not attain the bigger operatic roles, and would have to settle for a lighter repertoire altogether. A fine, versatile tenor (or a *heldentenor*) needs such nerve, muscle, temperament, and a *great stamina*, that it is not surprising that he is such a rare creature. Tenors are greatly in demand and a most precious vocal phenomenon.

Since I was a student and first heard the counter-tenor voice, much has developed in this genre. I heard Alfred Deller when I was very much a beginner and a soloist with Michael Tippett's group of singers and instrumentalists (meeting at Morley College). The impact of this unearthly and wonderfully musical line and tone was startling! Very soon many other counter-tenors appeared — seemingly out of thin air! Ever since then the growth, colour and expression of, and demands made on, this kind of voice have grown further than one would have though possible. This is exciting.

There is one kind of vocal unease which many prefer to overlook — indeed gladly — because of the great qualities that shine forth in some individual singers regardless of vocal method. I refer to those great vocal interpreters, who have a marvellously sensitive musical talent and response to words; also to certain fine actors. These are *personalities* with their very own, most personal sound, which may be incorrect and strained, even vocally creaky and scratchy, but beloved by their public. Their marvellous interpretive talent rightly overrides all else. Actors can live with strain *somewhat* more easily than singers because they use less range, less precision, less athleticism; and while breath support *must* be available, it can be less organized and perhaps a little less constant.

THE PLEASURES AND PERILS OF THE
SINGING PROFESSION

SOMETIMES I SIGH enviously as I consider the carefree
pleasure of the amateur choral singer, enjoying great music
as he or she takes part in one of our best national recrea-
tions, so far removed from the anxious world of the
professional singer — a world in which I feel deeply
involved, and heavily biased in my sympathies.

These days young singers have a more comprehensive
training than ever before: in music colleges and with post-
graduate opportunities, they are extended musically,
stylistically, dramatically, even gymnastically; and they
emerge equipped for battle — confident and brave. *Except*,
I find, in the vital area of vocal self-knowledge, where their
technique is not always sufficient to keep them steady as
their careers unfold and challenging demands are made on
them in perhaps unforeseen directions. How different from
the scene of young emerging instrumentalists, who develop
their techniques so fast and in such a frenzied fashion,
becoming wizards of dazzling speed and acrobatics, to a
point where often musical content dwindles to a mini-
mum.

There's much to say about the perilous paths in a singer's
life, also much to say about the pleasures that have bur-
geoned in the last ten years. One is the notion of presenting
the song repertoire as 'ideas' explored during an evening by
a group of well-chosen singers who cherish the music and
the text with great skill. This has brought in a huge new

audience. The Songmakers' Almanac, above all, have been brilliant pioneers in this field. Song repertoire and imaginative presentation have grown steadily since Graham Johnson brought this idea into being. An inspiration to us all.

Another pleasure is the ever-developing English National Opera: it has removed the musty old image that kept many away from this medium. Here is a great shop-window for talents of many kinds: a huge house with varying acoustics for singers to contend with — all part of the challenge. It bears a great responsibility in setting standards and, being adventurous, nurturing singers and bringing out their best and lasting qualities.

When I was a young singer one heard generalizations about singers having it all their own way, seeming to care exclusively for their own success in all situations. Later on it was the conductors who towered over the scene. Now it is surely the director who is omnipotent. Will there never be a balanced partnership between these forces?

The present-day imbalance between director and singer is worrying to many of us. A director of repute can draw the public into the opera house even over and above the composer, and his name may appear almost as the creator of the entire opera. Sometimes a producer's contribution is indeed important and stimulating — even inspired — bringing a new lease of life to music and libretto alike and stirring new thoughts in us. But too often a new production, whether in a large or small house, in the central scene or on the fringe, can actually shatter the wholeness of the music, and the listeners' concentration.

Instead of guiding our comprehension of the work we are confused by visual distractions and cross currents of ideas that fragment the music: the impression may be kaleidoscopic. No character or voice is allowed to develop into the listener's understanding. In the midst of activities that seem more of a self-indulgence than a communication, I have seen and heard singers struggling valiantly, striving to deliver a taxing role while contending with actions and positions that quite unbalance their basic alignment of breath and energy.

They have been singing while standing, or walking, or at times running, on a deeply sloping stage, up and down perilously, not just for a moment but for long scenes, disturbing their security from the feet upwards; or they have been singing from a dizzy height where a feeling of vertigo contends with control of the sound; they have been delivering difficult music while crawling on all fours — though that at least gives them a sense of balance!

On one occasion I noted an entire cast — for *Un Ballo in maschera* — all masked closely across cheeks and eyes — masked, throughout the opera, over a most sensitive area of expression, depriving those singers of an essential freedom, thereby reducing vocal colour, variety and resonance, and impeding their sound.

Sometimes leading ladies are required to sing lying flat on their backs, or slightly tilted up at the shoulders. This is not as difficult as it seems, since the body can still be in *its own* alignment. For the crux of the matter is that a singer should not be asked to ply his craft with his throat and supporting body *out of alignment*. An alignment is *the singer's absolute right*, as it is for every other instrumentalist. But because the singer's instrument is invisible, enormous advantage is taken of it. Indeed, I believe that some directors — especially in the area of music theatre — identify the singer's alignment as a lack of physical or emotional freedom, and believe that the correct response is to break the singer down psychologically in order to make him or her pliable on stage. This can be *dangerous*. Singers should not be 'undone' physically or emotionally. Their instrument is exceptional in that it is made to *carry emotional strength from within* and into the heart of their sound, needing a very particular alignment of energy, a strength not to be dissipated in other ways.

I have thought about this dissipation of strength when working occasionally with singers who have, at some time, been very advanced in sport or athletics. Their muscular strength and control was felt to be in their limbs, on the *outside* of their bodies. The struggle was to try to get their awareness of strength to work *inwardly* for their sound. I have also worked with several young singers who were enormously stout, with little wish to move about. Yet their stance was grand and their support *had* to be — and was — perfectly balanced, while their sound was concentrated, ringing, centred and expressive. Perhaps this is why over-weight is too often associated with good singing: it makes good stance and inner strength obligatory.

Meanwhile, I think it most unkind to young singers that, through the unhelpful indulgences of very many directors, their vocal excellence is no longer the first consideration in attainment of a role. Singers may now be chosen more for their personalities and 'allure' (of course important), or for their flexible ability to respond to a producer's ideas. And for their 'exciting' sound — a wonderful attribute, but one which today too often means 'excitingly in danger', inse-cure, a voice used rather as on a tightrope. The public responds to this feeling of tension, but must surely be bemused by the number of vocal techniques that they hear at any one performance.

An exciting world has been opened up by diverse experi-mental contemporary composers, with stimulating, daring ideas concerning human sounds. They make for humour and fun; and exacting dynamic schemes and time-patterns, written out with bizarre new-looking picture signs, can be attractive to young artists. These need do no damage to voices and are sometimes helpful extensions, so long as there is always an alignment of supporting energy throughout the performer's body. This can and *must* be managed whatever the requirements of composer, producer and conductor.

Franklyn Kelsey (in his book *The Foundations of Singing*) quotes the late Harry Plunket Greene remarking that whereas the "older composers wrote horizontally for the voice, the new ones tend to write vertically". Nevertheless, however 'vertical' the music, the singer must strive his hardest to keep his legato as 'linear' and 'horizontal' as possible, if only because the continuing health of his instrument depends upon it. The larynx is an instrument of *portamento*, and Nature cannot be persuaded to alter it in the cause of modernism.

The big influence nowadays is the fast-developing hugely popular 'music theatre', which blurs the edges of drama and music, attracting all manner of old and new talent. The training that goes with it, and into the opera house, by experimental producers, may require the singers to 'journey' from strenuous physical limbering into psychological exercise intended to liberate the personality. Some may respond gladly, but many become confused, or diffused and drained, losing the concentration that is needed to flow into the intensity of the emotional core of their sound. This is what the Bel Canto system was, and is, all about.

The larynx, our small precision instrument, is both remarkably tough and very tender. I am constantly amazed at how well it manages, how resilient and resourceful it is, even while being abused and pushed around! But not for ever. The signs of strain are shown not only in the singer's distress, but also in the oncoming unsteadiness of line, breathiness and then the uncontrollable waver.

However, young singers are more than willing to try all that is asked of them, and seldom complain, feeling that somehow they should be equal to all challenges, or else jeopardize their chances in the profession.

Some directors have studied singing themselves, but, whether or not they have, I wish that they would consider the very special requirements of the voice and go along with the singers' basic needs, encouraging them to find vocal emotion from 'within', not from 'without', and so honour, not debase, the coinage of our craft. Perhaps the very opposite of the callous way of treating the voice is to be found in the musical intention implicit in the vocal lines of Verdi's early operas — lines of intense drama where not even the orchestral accompaniment is allowed to distract with more than 'umpty-tumpty' chords — or in Monteverdi's deeply emotional vocal line, with next to nothing around it.

You may ask, "But where are the voices today which can manage to convey all this unaided by producers' effects?" Yet we have surely all heard fine voices — the sound of which enthrals us — voices we would not wish to burden with discomforts and distractions? I believe that trained voices, at whatever stage, should not be asked to extend their vocal boundaries beyond a certain limit, no further than can be contained within a true alignment of their own particular vocal system at that time. Singers can help defend their craft by finding and being aware of this alignment, which enables them, as I said earlier, to centre their energy into vowel tone and use it creatively. Singers carry that responsibility as well as producers.

The profession is certainly an exciting one! Finding work at all is an initial excitement and hazard, followed by developing and caring for the voice in the face of many adventures. The rewards are within the ever-widening scope for performance: new places, new ways, new groupings, new compositions, and the very early repertoire — and, above all a keen, expanding public.

SIDE TRACKS AND DECEPTION!

THE DIVIDING LINE between opera, grand opera, operetta, music theatre and many kinds of musical has become increasingly hazy in recent years. The new directors delight in developing their ideas in any and every one of these styles. Besides adapting themselves to the unvocal demands this trend often implies, which I bemoaned earlier, young singers these days must also be able to jump into many different styles and 'weights' of singing.

Up to a point it keeps them lively-minded and on their toes. But there is one new element in all this that is particularly confusing: the inclusion of electronic aids. When I was very young, in the early days of radio, the use of microphones was starting gently and insidiously, as were the developing skills of recording. One noticed what came through the air from singers' voices that we knew. Great voices (such as Flagstad's) did not sound so great: their most thrilling high notes had to be subdued, and their dynamic ranges were much reduced. And some of the least impressive voices, in fact the quieter and even hooty ones, came over best, without distortion.

My own singing, which deviated somewhat erratically from the steady line required, was very awkward for the radio knob-turners. The crooning pop singer of that time could be turned up and inflated from just a whisper into melting sensuality. A gritty, sexy Satchmo (Louis Armstrong) became compelling. This was the beginning of a whole new world of deception. Since then, mechanical skills have leapt ahead.

I have always felt that the beginning of the end of real vocal art would be the use of microphones in the concert hall and opera house. The balance and athleticism of the singer's true sound would thereby be compromised — would lose its bearings, balance and strength. The great operatic composers wrote for voices in such a way that the emotion could ring through the very core of the vocal system, from 'within' not from 'without'.

The voice is unique in being able, when in true alignment, to take over the depths, and indeed every shade of human feeling. Once it is unbalanced, inflated, confused, the situation becomes complicated.

I believe that this confusion is now upon us, though not obviously. The bigger opera houses *do* sometimes amplify their singers' sounds, though this is hardly perceptible when the microphones are at a distance from the singers.

The public does not usually recognize how confusing the voice scene now is. Generally, audiences go for what is on offer, whether human, part-electronic, adequate or exciting; ugly, emotionally true, beautiful as 'sound' ... or a serviceable noise.

The world of vocal and instrumental pop is even more of an electronic mélange. Musicals lace their sound with elaborate synthesizers, which sometimes take over a singer's vocal line while the singer mimes the sound unbeknownst to the audience. Every soloist will have a personal mike, usually in the hair, neck or bosom, with batteries concealed somewhere else. In this way vocal strain is relieved, and nine performances a week made quite possible. While the dynamic level or orchestral accompaniment may be crashingly loud, every musical show has an elaborate 'sound console' which is controlled by one expert who can mix, emphasize, stir around and reduce or increase any and every line of sound in that production. The balance is up to him. He can make or mar a performance. His influence is total — careers could be swayed ...

I have taught some of the soloists who sing in musicals. I emphasize the same basic skills that we *all* need: particularly the understanding of *support for the breath* so that no harm need be done, and often much pleasure experienced and given. But in the pop-rock-jazz scene, to which many turn their ears for release from a hard world, the vocalists are often *not really singers*. They tear their voices apart using the lowest register very high indeed, and quite hysterically at times, crying with frenzied urgency or crooning tearfully. The vocalist holds, embraces, clings to that microphone, and his own noises are transformed with fascinating deception. But maybe they feel no real satisfaction in using sounds not entirely their own, which may account for the frenetic amount of body movement they need to make.

Young children hear a lot of these sounds on and off television and they may try making the same sort of noises, but without electronic aids. When they go to primary and secondary school they may be asked, in singing class, to find their own considerably gentler sound. It is easy for them to decide that this sound is 'boring' or 'cissy'. To find their own sound needs a very confident and artful teacher, and these are now rare, many having lost their nerve over such matters and become diffident about *their* own sound, and so unable to demonstrate. It is a great loss, because children, when well-guided, have a surprising and easy range, and breath support too (unless they are inhibited for other reasons). They are missing a lot.

The advent of amplification could be another and perhaps final blow to the art of Bel Canto. I hope I am wrong.

During the 80s and 90s so much has changed in the singing scene. Between the jazz and many-faceted Pop Rock Music and the classical world there is a widening range of Music Theatre performance, mingling styles. All this makes good use of many gifted, versatile singers — actors and dancers — who might not have found work elsewhere. Vocal requirements range greatly, and most are aided with some form of amplification and the ingenious, ever-growing possibilities of computers.

There are now departments in the Music Colleges to teach all theatrical vocal skills: their comprehensive voice training includes, very clearly stated, the classical technique and other ways of using the voice, including the very popular 'Belting', which can be safely done for limited periods of time. This is done by bracing the body and neck muscles and allowing the larynx to ride high — please don't experiment without help!. It is thought that the operatic Classical Tenor uses this sound *briefly* at the top of his range in extreme moments of excitement. Belting is exciting, brash and even alarming — carrying far, but by its very nature, totally *unyielding*!

TEACHERS AND STUDENTS

YOUNG SINGERS TEND to change teachers quite often, in maybe misguided zeal, hoping for quicker successes. Or maybe following a colleague who has been luckier in competitions, festivals, auditions? There is now less inhibition about 'changing loyalties' than when I was young: rather like the more frequent movement in other current human relationships! Sometimes these are wise decisions but quite often irresponsible and panicky. There are no easy answers.

Sometimes students flourish in an ambience which gives confidence rather than definite tuition — and in this ambience they find their own strength without being hurried. Sometimes there are hang-ups which are other than vocal, which hopefully resolve in diverse ways other than direct tuition. I work with the hope that acceptance of *basic* technique may also resolve other problems in life and in the personality.

Singers in a hurry with no steadying guidance tend to make hard-edged powerful sounds: it is very difficult to dissuade them. I would try to add more 'space' around this shrill sound and so bring in more warmth and flexibility. In accepting this, singers will feel (at first) that they are losing out rather than gaining until their inner ear and 'feelings' adjust. I try and explain, and it is not easy, that we are working for a clear onset of sound which meets our supported breath. This will be our *own personal* sound — as personal as our appearance and our character! The sound issues from our open throats with no obstacles in the way of its journey. This sound is precious; it will grow and flourish. As the Bel Cantists so rightly believed: quality first and quantity will follow.

It is important to recognise that the great singers of the world are basically instinctive and do not know exactly what they do and could be upset by knowing. So it follows that they cannot be the best teachers. Yet, quite naturally they do attract great numbers of advanced student singers. There is a positive 'aura' around them and the 'sight' and sound of phrases demonstrated by them can be inspirational and lift the spirit and 'ears' of those around them. Attendance at their classes adds greatly to the prestige of those who were there.

In general what we hear around us has a great influence, and now, at the end of century, the general level of classical singing is high, even though confusing.

Singing 'coaches' are a very important part of singers' lives. They can do much to aid and abet difficult note-learning and then go deeper into interpretation and styles and use of foreign languages. But beware of those who take over from the singing teachers' craft in the realm of vocal technique — only *very* occasionally does this work! The profession of *coaching in depth* has grown since the end of the 30's, before the last war — led by Gerald Moore and the oncoming generation, and greatly encouraged by the skills of Paul Hamburger and other great musical talents (many of whom were refugees from Europe), and they in their turn have taught another generation — and have all uplifted the performance of singers immeasurably.

This book concerns the singer's *classical* technique rather than any other and, bearing this in mind, I do want to write once again about the importance and total usefulness of the 'Happy Surprise!' — that swift gesture which alerts the entire singer every time; at every breath; at every phrase, enabling the onset of the sound to take instant flight, with appropriate resonances.

The student usually finds this a very nice (and amusing) idea. We always include it in our practice, making friends with its 'feel', inside the mouth and open throat: the extra space and the 'cool air' at the soft palate as the breath comes in — the alert feel around the eyes and facial expression. But students do not always persist in *retaining* it into the muscular memory, sensing it in their speech and daily life. Recalling that the idea of this gesture derives from the Bel Cantists, I find no embarrassment in saying all this again.

I believe there are still confusing taboos at work in the teaching of singing. There is, for example, endless talk about 'focus', meaning, presumably 'where the voice is going', and very little about where it comes from. Focus is recognized very often as a sensation in the front of the face or head. But to teach awareness of where the sound is coming from, of the link between energy and the core of the sound at the larynx, is most unfashionable. I find this psychologically very interesting, because what people do when they link up with the core of their sound – something which the Mediterranean personality does so easily – is to meet up with the very heart of their emotional and sexual being. The Anglo-Saxon seems to have a resistance to something which goes so deep into the personality and requires so much physical and *inner* awareness. It feels to some like the exposure of a private realm. So they would rather believe that singing can 'just happen', that it is a mysterious impromptu affair, a knack which they find by accident (as some do), or else that it can be fabricated at another, shallower level that does not involve the whole person. Many singers perform pleasantly at this level and it can be appropriate in certain musical situations.

Of course, no singing teacher really knows what another is doing — we are all secretive, and many of us are frightened of others because we are so insecure. I have been a very insecure singer. But now, later in life, I am, rightly or wrongly, a secure singing teacher though forever questioning. I like to be challenged and I go to conferences always avid to hear more. My impression is that, whilst most teachers cover the area of breath support which is vital to all of us, and deal with various aspects of resonance, I am one of the few who insist that we discover the *core of the sound* simultaneously with high and forward resonance and its control.

But then, reports of what different teachers *do* teach are notoriously unreliable. Words mean such different things to different people. Our instrument is invisible and, to some extent, unfeelable. How are we to be understood? It is difficult, and I believe I have become more articulate over the years, but I know that my words may not be usefully understood by every singer however much I try to vary and adapt the images. I keep a check on mutual understanding by friendly questioning, and sometimes when singers report back on what we have done together, their words are confusing to me and I am distressed. But I accept that the sensations that go with their current choice of words may be valid: I must listen to what they are doing as well as to what they are saying and try to match up.

I have also discovered that my teaching about the core of the sound, about centering the voice, is something that my students don't often talk about. They'll tell others a lot of things that they've liked about their lessons, but they won't refer to vowel-centering. I think that this is all part of the already-discussed native resistance to using the voice as an expression of one's whole being. Sometimes excellent singers will even break away from lessons just at the very moment when they have joyfully discovered their centre and the sound is coming alive. It is as though the confrontation with themselves is too much to bear or too fragile to hold on to.

It is no coincidence that confidence is an enormously important part of singing. Without the physical buoyancy we feel when confident, the vocal system doesn't really work. But a lot of us have acquired confidence the wrong way. We have bought it cheaply, from a teacher who tells us we're 'all right', or even 'wonderful'. And this is such a comfort that we ride on it, some of the time — sometimes for a long time. I don't like to disturb a person who is in a state of confidence even if it is without foundation. If the technique is shaky, it is a delicate matter to suggest improvements, and only when pupils themselves feel that perhaps there are uneasy areas, can one quickly jump in to help.

Because of the nature of the profession, singers who are already in the swing of a career don't usually present themselves for lessons unless they are feeling either dangerously worn, or they have had some adverse criticism. And then one generally finds that one facet of the wholeness of their particular technique has been neglected. The resonances have, for some reason (perhaps through worry or depression), been partly cut off, or 'covered' by slackness in the facial expression, all of which is a burden on the larynx. If you cut off any one part of the whole system, then the larynx has to carry the burden. I find that singers who feel they are doing nicely in the profession, fear that lessons would be a disturbance. They are unwise. If they have sufficient confidence in their teacher, it is not a disturbance but a reassurance. And they all need constant —*constant*— reassurance. It is especially so in singing because singers cannot hear themselves as others hear them, and because the instrument is so incredibly variable and sensitive.

The intimate connection between voice and person is the reason why there can be no rules about how long training takes, and one cannot commit oneself, even in specific cases. Each student varies *so* much, and none would like to think of taking five, seven or even ten years or more before emerging in public, yet this is often the case. But anything is possible. There are all kinds of compromises, of course, but because we grow as people, and because of the frailties of our vulnerable instrument, most of us actually need to study and develop for *most of our lives*.

In my teaching I aim always to give confidence while unfolding the correct ideas about voice; to give *all freedom possible* as a result of working steadfastly at building the physical basis of the voice, at whatever pace life and the singer will permit.

Is there a recipe for a good or successful teacher of singing? It depends on so much, not least the occasional bonus of a 'born winner' dropping into his or her lap! For myself, I feel I could have done better, as a teacher, with a more neutral personality. Not too meek, but less strongly outgoing, insistent and excited than I tend to be. Some students can take it, and in consultations, workshops and master classes such a personality is invaluable. But as a steady presence one needs to be retiring much of the time. The students need to predominate, not to be over-awed, or over-persuaded, but to sort things out freely for themselves, with hints rather than commands coming their way. My strength — and difficulty — is that I *have* a 'method', though flexible. My conscience simply will not allow me to pretend otherwise, whatever the price. But 'methods' have a bad name. They seem to spell rigidity. Perhaps 'plan' or 'scheme' would be less threatening? Many years ago, during my interview for teaching at one of our principal music colleges I asked the Principal, 'Do you want to know about my way of working with voices?' The answer was, 'No, so long as you do not have a Method'. On one level I understood and sympathized. I made a wry smile and remained silent.

Above all, teachers should be *flexible* without losing essential beliefs, meeting each pupil wherever they are at that moment, even though it may be shifting ground. Never make a new student feel that they are *all wrong* and must start all over again, but that they will be able to *add* to what they already have, and that you will help them do so — sometimes when a student comes from another teacher there is a 'tussle' for a while, but more likely there is a 'honeymoon period'! As things steady, pupils need to find, recognise, feel and hear their new attainments (mutually approved with the teacher) and hold on until the muscular memory takes over.

If lessons together do not work out, neither party should feel guilty; try for an amicable parting of the ways rather than a divorce!

My lessons and classes follow a broad pattern: they nearly always start with limbering up the voice unless the singer feels really well 'warmed up', and then moving on to repertoire, bearing in mind the main points that have emerged from the limbering. The length and depth of the limbering will vary with each singer, but is always about 'making friends' muscularly with particular aspects of our craft, as described in this book. Endless variants can be thought out, but always based on the fundamentals described earlier. I do not count mindless la-la-la-ing as limbering, having done it myself uselessly over many years.

I have never played the piano at lessons except for an urgent chord here and there. I was a second-study pianist at music college but I have deliberately not developed piano playing for teaching purposes because I honestly cannot hear with the X-ray ears I need if I am searching for notes on the piano. Most teachers who play easily and accompany all lessons please their students at one level and also keep themselves happy and interested, however many hours a day they are at it. A bit of me finds this enviable, but I wonder if they really hear the singer 'in depth'?

Working without accompaniment is an exacting discipline for the student, but it is a way in which we can both judge exactly what the voice is doing — which is essential. Then, when we get near to auditions or performances, the singer and I choose one of the pianists we know to join us at lessons. Students usually like to bring a tape to the lessons: years ago I thought that this would be inhibiting for me but now I am totally used to it and welcome its presence! In addition, I like students to have sizeable note books and write up each lesson — its gains or losses? — new points and *particularly queries* — and their own comments and notes about the songs studied. Do they all bother to do this? No, I fear not!

I work at the 'content' or 'interpretation' of songs almost as soon as working technically — the two elements interplay all along the line. Whatever stage the singer is at, both are enriched.

Teaching Children

Some think that children's voices should be left alone till much later, but I believe that at every stage there is something helpful that can be taught to open up the singing and discourage shouting and straining! To encourage their sound and learn about good posture and clear words — gradually showing the way.

I have taught a great many boys and girls from the ages of

eight and upwards. If they are pleased about the lessons — and are not taking them only to please their parents — they are usually so natural and outgoing that our way of singing, based on a confident stance, a lively face and open throat, is there already or easily encouraged.

The idea of taking a breath as though 'happily surprised' comes *very* easily, and we can develop this into exercises much as I have described for all beginners. We also use words, making up sentences that suit our needs, or that amuse us, and it can all be fun and useful at the same time. When keeping the good all-over position, a surprisingly extensive range of notes emerges, often three octaves.

The disappointing aspect is the lessening of confidence and the more inhibited approach that gradually comes as the child reacts to school requirements and to restrictions of life in general, which surround him on all sides. Also, children who grow very tall, very fast (at around age twelve) tend to lose alignment of energy and buoyancy, their 'lower half' seeming to lose their 'upper half' (rather as Alice must have felt in Wonderland). But *most* of the time children can manage a well-harnessed overall strength that can support all their vocal needs.

Years ago I taught boy sopranos and altos who are much in demand by our main Opera Houses as soloists. They can learn to support and carry their voices without strain over an orchestra in varied demanding roles such as Miles in Benjamin Britten's *Turn of the Screw*, the shepherd boy in Wagner's *Tannhäuser*, the Spirits in Mozart's *Magic Flute*, and the shepherd boy in Puccini's *Tosca*. This kind of singing takes the '*whole*' of them — very much more so than does the lighter 'oo-ish' cooing sound so well suited to the acoustics and ambience of church and cathedral. This is a sound I do not actually teach — beautiful though it is. I like to encourage the more Italianate warmer sound as I heard it years ago in Westminster Cathedral — but at that time nowhere else.

Benjamin Britten also preferred this fuller sound when choosing the boy singers for some of his operas. I was lucky to be able to help train them through my work as a consultant teacher to the Finchley Children's Music Group — formed by the Andrewes family around 1970 onwards and playing an exciting part in musical life for many years. I also taught these boys privately and was able to follow through their development. Very few continue singing professionally in adulthood but all remain enriched musically. As their voices approach the 'breaking' time, between the ages of twelve-and-a-half and fourteen, lower notes emerge in speech and song, and also astonishing high notes, more ringing than ever! In fact I have heard such beauty at this time, enhanced by the boy's increased sensitivity at this age, that I seem to have 'glimpsed', maybe, the sound of the legendary castrato.

At this time the boys begin to feel their middle notes to be awkward and unsafe, yet if the skills they have learnt are working well, they can avoid 'bumpy' or 'collapsed' notes, and can even keep the break at bay a little longer, a few months maybe, and so delay 'retirement' from the public scene if there are very special performances to do at this point. When things get really awkward, a rest is indicated; and *ideally* the singing voice should not be used for at least six months. It is tempting for the boys to try out the lower 'grown-up' notes, and often their school will suggest singing tenor or baritone to help the choir. This is a question that must be left to the discretion of the boy and the teacher, but I myself would not encourage it.

Young girls do not have so many opportunities as soloists — nor do their voices 'break'; but instead their range of notes remains fairly constant though gradually more colour, more 'timbre' emerges as they enter the teen years. No 'resting' time is needed — but pressures should not be put upon them at this or any other time.

From my Lesson Notes
Among those who are making their way, there are many who are held back by the performance of the voice over and above the *passaggio*. Instead of flowering into their fullest expression and most beautiful sounds, something else is happening. It is a crucial area for all of us.

I worked with a fine baritone of excellent intelligence and musicality who also had outstandingly good looks, health and personal charm. Yet he was not getting to the professional level he should have reached. The sound seemed to be 'complete' in the middle area, but as it moved over and above the *passaggio* there was unease and some falling off of quality. Either the sound would 'thin out', developing a headier quality and losing the intention of the phrase, or he would *push* the voice out strongly, giving it a hardness that was not wholly acceptable. Both ways the listener was let down.

He was glad to work on this problem. We began, as usual, with gentle open-throated humming, awakening the feel of a high level of resonance across the top of the face and forehead. Then we carefully worked the start of the note exercise and took this 'fine start' into a vowel-centering exercise — the triad-plus-one — beginning on the same open 'a', gong to 'e' and 'i' and back to 'a' again. We began on middle C, worked down a little, and then up by semitones.

I asked him to free his whole self between each exercise. As he moved near and into the *passaggio*, I asked him to do *nothing different*, but to keep the position constant even though at a greater cost in muscular tension and concentration. I would urge him on enthusiastically with my own gestures and signs, so as not to stop the progression. If all went well he would not opt out, but *bear* with the situation of intensifying the vowel muscles at source, letting them take over with — I sometimes say — 'more reality' and definition of the vowel. On he went to the top of his range, as far as he felt he wanted, with *no stopping* en route to estimate how he was doing. The important part of this exercise was to keep a hold of the situation, proving to himself that the voice *could* take the muscular demands he was making, and take them *gladly*. The experience can be exhilarating, and with this singer it often was. All this is properly used *effort,* NOT *straining.* This can confuse the singer! I need to work on and explain how we need effort to develop muscles inwardly — not outwardly as we do in gymnastics. This is an area that may make singers uneasy, and the teacher needs to be very confident of what they are doing — as the laryngeal muscles learn to work for us, and strengthen, the 'bigger' muscles of relevant parts of the body join in, involving themselves naturally.

After some ten minutes (*not* more) of this, the student and I would take a short holiday by working at *agility*, light and free-wheeling. I would suggest the small five-note figure on 'laugh'. I asked him for a tall broad stance and wide-open throat allowing the larynx to bounce, or oscillate, which it will gladly do to deliver its special running knack. This we did throughout his range. Then we would return to a little more vowel centering over the crucial area. This time we began on G below middle C, with a small shape up and down, G B C B G, sung with intensity over the curve of the short phrase, with a *messa di voce (crescendo and decrescendo), feeling* the vowel, anchoring it deeply through these notes; binding the notes and allowing the vowels to lead.

My baritone liked to work over this area again with

muscles refreshed; now a little more limbered and ready to give more centre to his sound. Again, I reminded him to make no change in the technical plan: neither to analyse the sound, nor to 'cover' it, but just to enjoy the physical process of achievement — the control of the core of the sound.

If some notes were stubborn, refusing to ring, I suggested trying a brief *vibrazione* on these notes, which worked wonderfully.

This kind of limbering work needs real staying power. I have noticed that a singer who is very athletic outwardly, in sport, for example, does not usually find the *inner* strength and awareness needed for strength in singing — which is quite a different matter.

If a singer succeeds in strengthening the area of the voice that we are talking about, so that he may *carry true conviction*, then the outlook professionally may change greatly. The singer will be excited by what has happened. But to *live with it* is a big commitment. Some singers fight shy of this further discipline; though I have not heard them say so in as many words, I have sensed it. They remain on the periphery and never advance professionally quite as far as they could.

The singer I am remembering as I write achieved what was so much needed in the higher part of his voice during his sessions with me, to our mutual delight. But, sadly, he would let it go again, perhaps not able to continue working on his own so carefully, so intensively, and possibly not daring to use the new skill in public. Finally the matter seemed well established, but again, he 'let himself off the hook', went to another teacher with another angle, and the end of the story is still unknown to me.

But the *pattern* is not unusual. Another baritone I worked with, needing a similar kind of development in the *passaggio* area and beyond, is so near to great singing that he can drive discerning listeners frantic! His laid-back stance keeps returning after promise of so much more. The shortcoming is in the personality, not in the voice but in a deep-down lack of confidence and fear of a different future, maybe a fear of success? or maybe a fear of his own depth of feeling that might emerge with well-anchored singing.

There is a fine line between vocal excellence and 'alrightness' which is crucial and tantalizing. From the technical point of view there is no compromise in the way we have to work, as I understand it. The longer the singer performs with this kind of problem *unsolved*, the more rigid the voice becomes. This had gone on *so* long with another singer who worked with me in some distress, that his career had dwindled from front-ranking to nearly nothing. The crawl back again was a tremendous task — for body and soul. And a busy tenor I was asked to help preferred *not* to tackle it. So instead of developing into big Verdi leading roles, he switched to lighter 'buffo' types, for which he had plenty of equipment. The impasse was thus avoided with a very happy outcome. This showed me that not every singer is obliged to keep his entire range in pristine condition. He is at liberty to cut his cloth to suit his coat, finding his niche in a style that suits his temperament and reduces anxiety; and in this particular case to very great success!

One of the finest sopranos I have worked with felt, at the age of twenty-five, that she had come to the end of the road. She had sung naturally and successfully from the age of nine or ten, winning prizes all the way: competitions, festivals and scholarships. When we met she had just received another accolade, yet she had a feeling that the voice had nowhere to go or grow. And, at that moment, it was true.

To start again, yet continue in her career, was a big challenge for both of us. Happily, the basics of the method in which I believe, helped instantly. The open throat, resiliently maintained, and the feeling of space around the voice, was a new notion for her. Naturally, her throat had been *instinctively* open much of the time. But at tricky moments it had closed, and she had pushed her sound forward, somehow, into the mask, the nose, or somewhere where it could no longer bloom and by so doing had lost the alignment with her body support.

We worked a great deal on encouraging 'space', and within this 'scaffolding' we found the centre of vowels, with *no* closing or squeezing of the position allowed. The feel of high resonance was also never forsaken. Her breathing and support were already working well. *Vibrazione* and *messa di voce* were tonics for her. Our usual exercises were extended where she most needed to work, and were practised diligently. Her career developed quickly.

I worked for a year or two with another young lyric soprano performing leading roles in one of our main opera houses. I was asked to try to help her over what seemed to be a very bad patch. The voice was deepening, the higher notes hardening. The 'ease' at higher levels was fast disappearing. She felt very scared and uneasy, developed thick catarrh and cancelled many performances. The opera house, not wanting to lose such a talented performer, planned mezzo roles for her.

Our task was to work for a new *feel*, bridging the developing lower warmer sounds with the top, gradually finding a new, comfortable approach. As usual, we worked from a correct 'start of the note' into the centre of vowels, so that she could find an anchor throughout the range. She needed to become aware of the totality of the working of her voice whatever the *tessitura*. After some months a new phase in her career began which has since blossomed into a fine international career, and in many styles.

A young soprano aged twenty-four appeared after a

music-college training in South Africa. She had just finished her course, but, instead of feeling well-equipped, she realized with dismay that she could not manipulate her huge voice at all. She could neither lighten it nor vary its colour; nor could she use it with any agility. Her own pressure was such that there was already a heavy undulating waver.

She had the courage to start all over again once she had found the teacher and the recipe. Reversing a waver (and oncoming wobble) is one of the hardest things for the singer and the teacher. Mercifully, she and I both had determination and patience for as long as was needed. All the essentials of this method were urgently needed. The muscles that govern *vibrazione* and *messa di voce* are crucial: we limbered on all kinds of shapes, from small ones to much bigger and more ambitious arpeggios.

I encouraged her to become *inwardly aware*, so that the anchor of sound was *tangible*. The support of the breath had to be constant but not rigid or *pushed*. Some vowels needed more persuasion than others to keep in line. The 'o' vowel, as with so many singers, was difficult and needed 'capturing' from the vowel preceding it, with that feeling of intense binding of notes. Above all, we had to find balance between the vowel centre and the breath at the point where they meet yet still mingle with high resonance and 'ping' or 'ring'.

Then, we also sometimes needed to switch away from concentration on vowels to the freedom for agility and the *trust* this needs. Extracts from arias by Rossini were ideal for this work, affording repeated situations of intensifying for a moment and then releasing into a melisma — all demanding a more pliant breath support from her and also, of course, less anxiety.

This kind of *arduous* work is constantly cheered on its way by Nature's amazing response to a system which feels *right* and comfortable. The muscles gratefully re-form and build a new muscular memory. I believe that it is also essential to keep cheerful by using *interesting* exercises, songs and arias (or bits of them) that appeal to the singer. The 'waver' comes from an imbalance, over-pushing and over-taxing the fine edges of the vocal chords, and it is somehow a sign of the times — so many young singers are trying to make too much noise, and the whole environment of the profession is pushy: endless auditions and competitions and not enough work for all the talent there is. It is also true to say that the singers most endowed with temperament and drive may be the first to fall victim, especially with indifferent teaching.

This young singer is now recovering slowly. It has taken a very long time because she has carried a problem through many years from her dancing training in Music College: very stiff stomach muscles — a constant 'drawing in' to a point of rigidity. How to let *this area* relax yet keep the rest of the supporting muscles alert and elastic takes a lot of understanding and skill. Without flexible lower tummy muscles we cannot use them freely, as we constantly need to do — I confess to having been baffled, though I dealt with it in agility exercises to some extent. I now find that I can keep my own rib cage lifted and broad and yet have free stomach muscles — I often check on this in my daily life.

Workshops and Master Classes

Startling things can happen in class situations. With amateur workshops, all present who wish to sing have a try: some have a craving to perform coupled with a huge fear of the unknown. There can be exhilaration, a great sense of achievement, but sometimes total collapse. If one fosters goodwill and pleasure in all that transpires, the listeners are as excited with the quick progress of others as with their own. However, involved listening *before* performing is difficult for singers. Meeting each day for, ideally, five or six days, at least gives each singer a second chance to sing again and to develop their first venture and more, after talk and suggestions and the melting down of tensions.

For example, an ardent chorister, a baritone who seemed well set-up as he prepared for his solo, was instantly galvanized physically into a defensive stance when he began to sing — as though he were being shot at! He kept this horrible stance up throughout the entire song. I used frank words as well as my hands physically to undo the knots, and he was relieved to find a possible alternative. With his friendly personality, he agreed with himself and all at the workshop to adopt a more relaxed stance. The result was sheer relief and joy for him, and for his listeners no less.

A mezzo had listened for a week to the same class a year earlier, not daring to sing herself. She was an amateur folk singer 'only' and couldn't relate to other songs (so she had thought). That year she returned with resolution and Handel's 'He shall feed His flock'. Her way with this had the ease, warmth and sincerity of a folk song — musical phrases, words to be shared — which delighted all present. She had an alert expression, an unlocked throat and some buoyancy in her stance, and was able to make good use of Nature's technique at her own level.

A timid lady chose a most *fervent* song: 'Er der Herrlichste von Allen' and lost every ounce of commitment by collapsing physically all over it, sounding as though she were in mourning. A later attempt, however, with suggestions on how to stand and to bring lower tummy muscles up to 'meet' the expression, made her version acceptable and more satisfying to us all.

Master Classes differ from Workshops only in the degree or depth of work that can be brought to them both by the soloist and the teacher ('Master'). The soloists, at whatever level of expertise, will have prepared their offering and the teacher will be ready to meet them at that level and will hope to take them further. If the mood of the class is happy and positive, which I feel is *essential*, much can be achieved. If not, there can be a kind of intimidation that freezes all concerned, even though the teacher may feel on top of the situation. Listeners can help enormously by their presence. During helpful classes there can be astonishing leaps forward — new insights, new skills show themselves. The gains may not always remain consistent afterwards, but the glimpse is always an inspiration for work ahead.

MORE ABOUT BEL CANTO

THE CONVICTIONS I now have about the voice have come insistently out of my own long years of vocal frustration and, finally, from enlightenment brought about by ideas already so well tried in the past, but recently in shadow. For this reason, I want to write a few more lines about Bel Canto, the early Italian school of singing to which I owe everything — as do countless others, often without being aware of it.

All my life I had heard those two words, Bel Canto, mentioned, usually with a sigh as though referring to a bygone, unattainable wonder; or mentioned with an unassailable assurance, as though only the speaker fully comprehended their magic meaning. In fact the term Bel Canto — 'beautiful song' — reflects work done by musicians in Italy during the seventeenth and eighteenth centuries who investigated the cultivation of solo singing as an art. The movement began in Florence, and soon spread to other Italian cities. It may have been prompted by the polyphonists, led by Palestrina: their use of separate expressive vocal lines woven together called for musically emotional sound as never before — a kind of vocal orchestration.

Soon the newly enriched solo voice began to dominate. Polyphony declined and harmony developed as accompaniment to the voice which now needed, even more, its own instrumental personality — a core, or definition to the sound. Together with such a core, florid, agile, colourful coloratura singing developed, in which the soloist had much musical and vocal liberty. Expressive vocal embroidery became the hallmark of the artist, as distinct from the skilled craftsman. By the time of Gluck, this freedom had gone even further, and the singers probably became very competitive.

The work of the Bel Cantists, those who researched and taught voice in the early days of the movement, was guarded. It was not generally published, and the training they advocated was based on very long and thorough lessons with one teacher, taking perhaps as much as ten years. Some of the secrecy was broken — luckily — by a few teachers who wrote books or articles, or published their exercises. Alessandro Busti was one, and — much later — Gaetano Nava (c. 1860), another who published his exercises. There was also Porpora, known to be a great teacher, whose work was written down by Isaac Nathan. Composers in the Bel Canto circle revealed, by their compositions, what they wished the voice to express, and most sang themselves, including Cavalli, Monteverdi, Carisimi and Rossini.

In the early part of the twentieth century, the singer and teacher Manuel Garcia was still working within the Bel Canto tradition. However, his invention of the laryngoscope, though an exciting step forward, could then offer only a distorted view of how the mechanism behaved. And his emphasis on the 'coup de glotte' was badly named and misunderstood. Nevertheless, he remains one of the great figures in the Bel Canto story.

Another link with Bel Canto, for the sensitive ear, are a few of the earliest of all gramophone records, made during the first years of this century. In spite of primitive sound mechanics, a special vocal tone and approach can be heard. One such record is that of Dinh Gilly singing Caccini's

'Amarilli'. Another is Fernando di Lucia's 1904 recording of 'Ecco ridente in cielo' from Rossini's *Barber of
Seville*.

It is fascinating to know that Sir Henry Wood was
Garcia's pianist at lessons given at the Royal Academy of
Music in London. Henry Wood picked up the great essentials in Garcia's teaching and used them in his excellent and
witty books on singing (the final one, called *The Gentle Art
of Singing*). His simple instruction, 'Say the vowel at the
cords', tells us very clearly how to go about it and gets to the
heart of the system, which was also excellently summarized
in Franklin Kelsey's article on voice in Grove's Dictionary
of Music – 5th edition.

Paraphrasing Kelsey's article, one realizes that the Bel
Canto school is one of intensity of voice as opposed to
volume of voice. It is a school of vocalizing 'at the larynx —
the power station' as part of an act of coordination. 'At the
larynx' means that the voice is 'upon the breath' as opposed
to the more modern concept of 'mingled with the breath'.
As a forerunner to this, the Bel Canto approach involved a
complete departure from the habitual machinery of speech
— unlike the *parlando* school of singing which probably
preceded it, and which has certainly succeeded it.

The entire Bel Canto system was built upon the isolation
and continuous 'caress of the glottis', the all-important act
which took precedence over breathing, tone amplification
and articulation. Through an understanding of *vibrazione*
and *messa di voce*, both of which depend on isolation for
their successful operation, the exclamatory vowels could be
used in every shade and grade to produce colouring appropriate to the mood and emotion expressed — all worked
from the energy imparted to the sound-waves at the source
of their vibration.

This method did not attempt to interfere with the natural

behaviour of sound, but allowed it to radiate outwards with no propulsive assistance from the singer. The Bel Cantists understood that sound cannot be pushed by breath-pressure. Although many singers and teachers know this old and fundamental principle of Bel Canto, and that the text must be expressed by means which are mainly musical, there has been serious confusion for nearly one hundred years. Since the vocal world turned away from tonal intensity (i.e. what scientists call 'radiation efficiency') and attended instead to *volume* of tone, ill-advised medical opinion, with little knowledge of sound physics, has supported some very misleading ideas. To step up vocal power the medical 'experts' extolled the low stomach breath, thereby preventing the diaphragm's vital freedom to compress the breath towards the larynx. Then came new theories focusing attention on *placement*, not maintaining the act of singing at the instrument, but placing it in some nook or cranny of the head. This altered the entire conception of singing, which thus gradually lost its instrumental character and became a more specialized extension of the normal speech faculty.

The insights of Bel Canto could only have originated in a Mediterranean country where outgoing people spoke a language built around open vowels — vowels allowed a 'life of their own', in a speech habit with a resilient bounce to it. Far as this may be from our colder, more reserved climate, I sincerely believe that the Bel Canto system really got to the heart of the matter, and that we can — still — do best by following it.

Franklyn Kelsey's book on singing technique (based on his ideas about Bel Canto), *The Foundations of Singing*, is one of the best, and the following paragraphs, quoted from it, show the depth of his understanding.

Where is the laryngeal diapason which was the blood and bone and muscle of the older art? Indeed and indeed, we have lost something!

There is no single act of vocal technique more vital, or of greater importance, than the gesture of the larynx which the true singer employs in order to launch the sound.

The effect of the old kind of singing, which is based upon the larynx instead of the vowel cavity, is to obliterate completely the differences caused by accidents of language, and to put every aspirant to vocal honours, of no matter what nationality, on to the same starting line. It takes longer to learn because it involves a complete departure from everyday speech habits; but once learned, it not only brings out the full beauty of the instrument, but also ensures its longevity. In his autobiography (*Student and Singer*) ... Santley records his frequent distress, as a student, at the smallness of his voice. The vocal development which took place as a result of his training enabled the possessor of that small 'pipe', as he himself called it, to become a Vanderdecken unsurpassed to this day for sheer sonority of tone. The voice is, in the first place, *a set of muscles* which our English habits of speech do nothing whatever to develop. True singing is as much a gymnastic exercise as ballet dancing, and when it is practised skilfully, there is no end to the possibilities of development. Teach English men and women to use their larynxes, instead of, as now, abusing them, and the world is liable to be very astonished at the size of English voices. We shall begin to hear once again something of the lost laryngeal diapason! ...

The best teachers in the world cannot make singers of pupils who are unwilling to learn slowly, for of all musical instruments, the human voice is the most unamenable to control, and is almost unique in being subject to mental influences of a rebellious nature. Every period of learning must be followed by a period of mental assimilation, so that each step is secured before going on to the next.

It must be taught skilfully and correctly, or left severely alone.

Nevertheless, there is no running away from the fact that he who cannot teach it cannot teach true singing, for it is the sole means which the singer has at his disposal *for launching a tone which has not an undesirable content of unphonated air.*

A vowel-sound is throaty because it is trapped in the throat, and not because it is formed in the throat.

Whenever the singer produces a note in this way, he has complied with the real meaning of Crescentini's aphorism: 'The Italian school [of singing] is a school of the voice above the breath,' for he then perceives that his voice is being made, not in the mouth, but somewhere below the throat, where the breath ceases to be 'breath' and becomes voice.

CHOIR TRAINERS

As I write now in the late nineteen-nineties, the level of much choir singing is so superbly high, that this chapter may well seem an impertinence! But in case some of it is still true enough to be useful I will continue. This time I am adding suggestions for warming up the voices before rehearsals — all of which are adaptable to the needs of singers and trainers.

Those in charge of school singing and the training of amateur choirs show an alarming lack of knowledge of the human voice. A trained music teacher at all levels is expected to be able to play the instrument that he teaches; yet in the subject of singing, with which he may have to deal every day, the teacher is not expected to know about the workings of the voice. No qualifications are asked for, and very little training is included in the teacher's course. Yet children are at the mercy of this situation at an age when their voices are very vulnerable. As well as occasional hymn singing, they take part in ambitious concert programmes — often for the benefit of the school's prestige. Musically this may indeed be a fine experience, yet vocally it can be harmful.

With honourable exceptions the picture in choral singing, at school and outside, is something like this: the choir plunges into rehearsal without warming up the voices, because there is no knowledge of how this very important voice-care should be undertaken. So, with an eye on the clock, because time is always short, the choir is asked to tackle the job in hand; maybe in full voice. This may involve learning — reading the notes of an as yet unknown section of a work — which means trying to find the right position in the voice-box whilst pitching notes uncertainly, which is very taxing. Although the larynx and vocal folds are remarkably tough, real damage can be done by vocal thrusting into unknown intervals, instead of a light, heady tone being used for this endeavour. Then, as the music becomes more familiar, the singers are asked for 'expression' and various dynamic shades, with no knowledge of the proper way of achieving such effects. They try to oblige, often 'pushing out' voice and breath, knowing little about supporting the voice, thus merely throwing more strain on the larynx and vocal folds.

Sometimes a conductor is sensitive enough to conjure up images which evoke the right responses and so produce unstrained singing, which is a great asset; but this is rare. Church-choir trainers may feel I am being unjust. Admittedly, they usually encourage a light, rather hooty 'oo-ish' sound which, although lacking in variety and colour and in the ability to develop, is certainly not such a strain on either the choristers or the teacher as the 'pushing' of amateur choir sound. But they, too, need to use a more consistent support of the voice through a proud stance.

Connected with all this is the frequent misuse of their own voices by teachers addressing school classes. Teachers are more sinned against than sinning. Working through thirty or more years of depending on their own speech as the prime tool of their profession, without any training at all in how to use and project their individual vocal potential. In the course of their school life they often become prone to intense anxiety on account of their speaking voices, and may even panic at difficult moments in large or unruly classes. Many children speak lazily and in a 'deadpan' fashion — whatever their background — but they cannot be influenced towards anything better by teachers who themselves are flummoxed or embarrassed with their own sound.

In choir rehearsal, however advanced the singers are musically, they will always need some warming-up exercises; these are simple ways that will get the muscles going gently and quickly and if planned carefully need take no more than ten minutes.

Here are some suggestions for Choir Trainers and voice leaders who conduct any and every sized group of voices. If possible sing along with the choir in areas of the voice comfortable to you.

Standing Tall and proud is always a good start and in the long run is less tiring than slouching. Head tall, breast-bone area braced — back muscles and lower tummy muscles alerted.

Shoulder rolling: 'over, back and down' in your own time — for two minutes?

Try some *light, happy, open vowels, unpitched*, all over the range, in your own time: a e i o u (a veritable fruit salad of sound) with a feel of space and an open throat — a gesture of 'happy surprise' as described earlier in this book. This alerts the whole person in one or two minutes and usually brings with it a smile and a good mood —

'a' as in sun
'e' as in yes
'i' as in sing
'o' as in not
'oo' as in moon

Next some 5 note runs — taken up to and beyond their

usual range of higher notes, with ever more feeling of 'stretch'. Light, bouncy, agile: your choice of vowels keeping the 'o' and 'a' for your higher notes. A chord played between each exercise as you transpose up or down — again with a light spacey feel: more an 'implosion' than an 'explosion'. Reaffirm the open spacey feeling at each new breath after a brief relaxation (the 'Happy Surprise'). Extend the exercise over the octave when you wish — an octave scale plus one tone and down.

Next, an *arpeggio of ten notes* using all the vowels as required — mf and pp alternately. The 'e' vowel helps *lift* any slight flatness, the 'o' and 'oo' encourage warmth but tend to droop in intonation — even a *thought* of the 'e' vowel can pick them up.

Include a *humming phrase* at some point in the limbering, encouraging a high level of resonance with a feel of 'Buzz' across the cheeks and eyes — nostrils flared! All lower pitches need a touch of what I call the 'speaking sound' blended in — a nice mix preventing a sudden drop into chest sounds and with body support well sustained.

Please don't be shy of demonstrating or leading the choir in the area of your voice *where you feel comfortable*. For the rest, your gestures of direction and approval will be enough.

Finally, when your choir sits, let it be 'Tall and Proud'!

FINALE

I HOPE TO have led you towards a way of unlocking your voice so that the appropriate muscles are free to respond to your requirements, backed up by your entire body-energy, in harmonious combination, which brings practical results and contentment.

I came to this way of thinking and working late in my singing life, and with immense relief — but not, unfortunately, with the kind of time necessary to use it professionally for myself. My ardour was and is directed instead towards opening doors for others, whoever and wherever they may be, convinced that we should all have a chance to get it right, and so develop our individual sound from that point.

Thus we can feel the inner balance exactly where breath becomes sound and in the spaces from where resonances can build. We need to be aware of the place in our throats where sound is initiated, and we need not be nervous of this awareness, which has for so long been somewhat taboo. This particular 'feel', together with the feel of the *all-important switchboard area across the top of the nose–eyes–cheeks*, is of the greatest benefit and both are interdependent. I have tried to describe nature's way of unlocking the voice. It feels and it sounds right, personal to each one of us.

The Bel Cantists lived in a spacious age, when singers could develop very slowly; but, even with the restless way of life today, we can still *find* ourselves and our sound by giving our devoted attention and our courage to the task. I believe that professional singers should build endlessly and ever more athletically on the foundations described in this book, needing greater awareness as the muscles develop, carrying their skills onwards with vitality and joy. Teachers of singing today who believe in this kind of approach to the voice are not many. So I have chosen three teachers who, although *far from modern*, are so full of good sense and insight, that I quote from them liberally as we draw near to the close of this book. I have already drawn attention to the work of Franklyn Kelsey. Sir Henry Wood, originator of the Promenade Concerts, whom we do not usually associate with singers, also wrote, with fervour, humour and excellent down-to-earth good sense, in several singers' manuals.

Franklyn Kelsey was senior coach at the Royal Opera House when I was a student and writes deeper truths on the voice than any other teacher known to me. Lucie Manén, whose excellent first book, *The Art of Singing*, was written when I and many colleagues were studying with her, published a revised version entitled *Bel Canto* which includes her further findings. I leave you with some more interesting and amusing quotations.

First, Sir Henry Wood in *The Gentle Art of Singing* (1930):

The besetting sin of the *modern singer is over-blowing*. As he strives to make a poor, thin voice into a big, warm, resonant one, he overtaxes his natural vocal physique, and his voice in consequence is generally unsteady, wobbly, breathy, with a dull, veiled, hooty quality. It is only a bright, clean tone which really carries over an orchestra in a theatre or concert room. Ring in the tone is the great quality for which to work. There should be vital life in the tone ... Fundamental vocal tone should always be bright, clear, clean, intense and ringing. And this takes many years of careful listening and diligent practice to obtain. We have no use in the singing world for dull, hooty, foggy, phlegmy, breathy tone. In fact, it is ring in the tone which distinguishes the highly trained, cultivated voice from the merely pretty amateur voice.

Finally, do not imagine that a singer's path is paved with gold or that it leads through green and flowery places. Reflect on the petty jealousies and intrigues of professional life, the great fatigue of constant travelling, the rehearsing in a cold concert-room after a long railway journey, a rehearsal which lasts a whole afternoon and leaves, perhaps, one hour for changing and swallowing a meal before the evening concert. Never mind in what country you mean to sing, without a strong will, immovable determination and the pluck of the devil, it will be hard indeed for you to win through and make good.

Given the material, rightly chosen, the process of training the singer begins. And here in modern times there is an essential defect in the shortness of the time given to training. We know that in the old days singers were students for six or seven years before their vocal physique was developed. Now you will find a singer expecting a paid engagement after he has had two singing lessons a week for a couple of years. Would any violinist think he could attain to proficiency on his instrument by sobbing out some emotional, slow-moving drivel every day for a year or two? Yet it is by exactly analogous methods that thousands of singers seem to believe they can reach the final goal of the vocal artist. You ask such people to sing a simple Handelian diatonic run and they come hopelessly to grief.

For the first three months it might be as well to give two or three minutes every morning, before starting your day's work, to fixing your thought upon your reed or vocal cords. Many students seem not to know where their tone is formed. They are able to think of head resonance, mouth resonance, throat resonance, neck resonance, chest resonance, but have only the vaguest notion of reed control ... Isolate your thought and will on the one spot, on your vocal cords. The following little exercise, which was well known to the old Italian masters, will help at this point, directing the student's will and thought to his tone-producing reed.

Take the symbol S (*don't* call out the name of the letter, just visualize it) which to a vocal student means a very light *pianissimo* stream of unvoiced breath, and during the light hissing of this symbol S, suddenly think and will the symbol Z (again, visualize it but don't call out its name), thus:

S_____   Z_____
a stream of unvoiced breath —   a partial approximation of
a hissed consonant.   the vocal cords — a buzzed
 consonant.

Do not increase the very light steady breath stream in passing from S to Z.

Do this little exercise half-a-dozen times; the mind will thus become conscious of where the vocal tone is produced, and the singer's attention will be concentrated on the cords. Much time is wasted at early singing lessons in trying to get tone into the head or chest, as though tone could be moved. Tone can be reflected, but it cannot be placed, either in the head or in the boots.

By willing your vocal cords (which are apart, during the symbol S) to partial approximation, you reach the buzzed consonant Z. See that you sustain this Z sound, without break or jerk. If the tone stops, flies off or dries up, it is that your thought and will-stream is not uninterruptedly directed, is not evenly continuous on and at the reed. This will probably happen the first time or two you try this exercise, giving S——z——s——z——s——z——Z——

Go a step further and turn your second symbol Z into a vowel — 'er' will do — and do this by thinking and willing your cords to tighten up and come together. The result will be a singing vowel.

The complete exercise of three parts will therefore be:

S_____	Z_____	Er_____
a stream of unvoiced breath — hissed consonant.	a partial approximation of the vocal cords — a buzzed consonant.	vocal cords, willed together, giving a continuous vibration: result — a vowel, *i.e.* voice.

Next, Lucie Manén in *The Art of Singing*:

Singing is the artistic expression of human emotion in sound. The expression of emotion is a reaction to internal and external stimuli in which the whole system participates: facial expression, gesture and attitude and vocal exclamations, together with heart-beat and breathing, reflecting the internal state of the individual. These reactions occur as reflexes. From the sensory organs — eyes and ears — impulses are carried via the nerves to the muscles which produce attitudes and gestures, to the muscles controlling facial expression, to the muscles of the larynx governing exclamations, to the centre of breathing and to the centres controlling the heart-beat. Chemical substances are poured into the bloodstream to supply the system with all those resources on which the human being unconsciously calls in any given state of emotion, be it hatred or love, joy or pain, surprise, fear or aggression.

In any such state of emotion the exclamation of the human voice follows laws common to human beings of all races. For describing events with little emotional content and in a neutral mood, the human voice uses exclamations in its lower range. As soon as the individual changes the emphasis of what he speaks or sings, the pitch of the voice changes. It rises with increasing emotional content. For the expression of pleasure the natural exclamation is 'a'. The exclamation 'ee' denotes disgust and hatred, whilst 'oo' denotes fear and horror. These are the basic exclamatory vowels.

In the golden age of Bel Canto, the seventeenth and eighteenth centuries in Italy, most composers of vocal music were also performing singers. They composed with an understanding of these inborn laws of the voice, using exclamations of every grade and shade as the foundation for their compositions, and their singing was based on the use of exclamatory vowels to produce colourings appropriate to the mood which the music was meant to express.

During the course of time the situation changed. Composers as a general rule are no longer singers, and the inborn laws of the voice are no longer known or sensed by them. Indeed, for many modern composers the voice provides simply one tone of a certain pitch in various intensities.

The internal make-up of the singer has changed also. Man has been taught and has learned to hide external signs of emotion. A schism has developed between vocal tone and emotion. This situation has been further aggravated by performing without an audience in radio or recording studios, where tones can be produced without the simultaneous facial and emotional expression. Singers have moved further and further away from the unique power of the voice to produce vocal colouring based on the exclamatory vowels as a means of interpretation — loud and soft tones replace changes of mood, and frequently singers today use only one of the potentialities of their vocal organ — one timbre — according to their own psychological make-up.

And finally here are a few of my own thoughts after fifty years of excitement and concern with singing.

What I have felt to be so important has not always been popular, so that there has not been success in a worldly sense, but I have been lucky in that I could nevertheless soldier on, working and learning all the time, and never feeling less than joy when singers find their way through technique into musical understanding and communication — a joy which is invigorating!

Research is now being done into every aspect of the voice — made possible by the new sophisticated appliances which allow the experts to observe the workings of the larynx and more, while the voice is actually being used.

All kinds of therapy are now possible — new learned books appear — some seem confusing but nonetheless important. Science seems to be on our side; affirming the instinctive know-how of correct singing — reaffirming the old with the new.

As singers move on and into the profession they may find all of it a daunting jungle! They need great drive to struggle through — there can be shattering times! I salute all those who keep going.

We teachers need to keep a positive relationship, whatever transpires. The singers' long-lasting achievements depend on an amalgam of a finely balanced vocal quality, good health, good luck, good looks, goodwill and a sense of humour! But above all, a compelling wish to communicate and share unreservedly the message of music and words with all their listeners at all times.

The magic then begins to unfold!

APPENDIX

Analysis of Schubert's
AN DIE MUSIK

THE THEME OF this song is thankfulness to music. Sing it at a moment in your programme when your composure is steady enough to transmit through the song to your listeners. Your vocal line begins quietly and grows steadily through each verse until the highest phrase. This phrase is then repeated devotedly as the thought and the verse come to rest. A legato line needs to be carried steadily on through whatever vowels you are singing, some with more weight than others.

The longer your vowels, the better the line and the clearer and more brisk your consonants. As I write about phrasing, I remember my friend Beata Popperwell (the eminent coach and pianist) reminding me that singers as well as instrumentalists need to take special care, not only in building the phrase with its pulse and momentum, but also in maintaining the energy as they 'bow out' of its shape.

Your thoughts need to be 'ahead' of you in direction. Allow the piano to take over the vocal line in the breaks between your phrases. Your tone should be constantly warm, whatever the dynamic; warm with sincerity, nothing contrived.

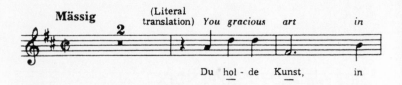

Move your thoughts and your sounds closely from vowel to vowel exactly as you *mean* them to sound, not 'singer's vowels', but 'for real', with rather more weight on the ones that carry your message.

I have marked the vowel sounds that need your attention, allowing the final syllable to lighten when appropriate.

Even as the lines descend, keep your feel of a 'high level of resonance' always spacey and available, so that as you move towards the higher phrases there will be no sense of rising strain.

The intervals like this one, 'du mein', should feel as though the notes are linked with a sense of 'drinking' or 'suction' behind the voice which keeps the throat resiliently open allowing the mechanism to bind the sound, *feeling* like a portamento, and sounding right and in line. Feel 'space' as the phrase rises and inner energy to carry you buoyantly over 'warmer lieb' …

Where there is a cluster of consonants like 'lebens winder' and 'kreis umstrickt', and others that I have marked, move *speedily* from the vowel before to the one after; this will sharpen and also clarify the intervening consonants.

This final phrase is quieter but needs more intensity — don't let it float away.

For this phrase, a sound that is gentle — intimate … Dwell on the *first* part of the diphthongs: 'seufzen'; the 'o'; 'deiner'; the 'a'; the second part of the diphthong will 'sing itself'.

Keep throat *open* between 'süsser' and 'heiliger'. Use the feeling of suction (S), as described earlier.

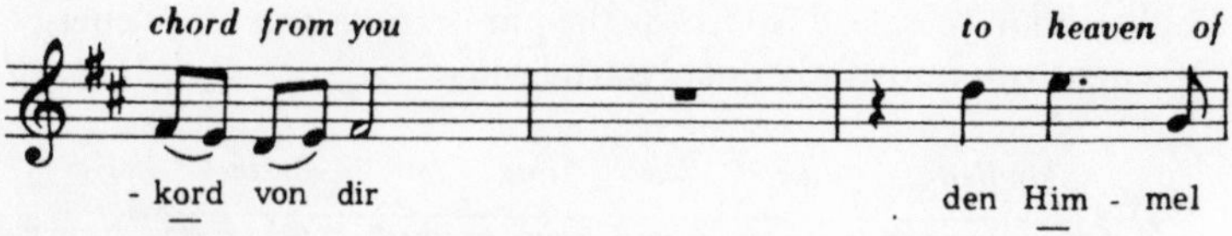

Pace this phrase: 'den Himmel' ... so that you can sweep easily over its peak. Here again is an interval needing to be connected with a feeling of suction or drinking.

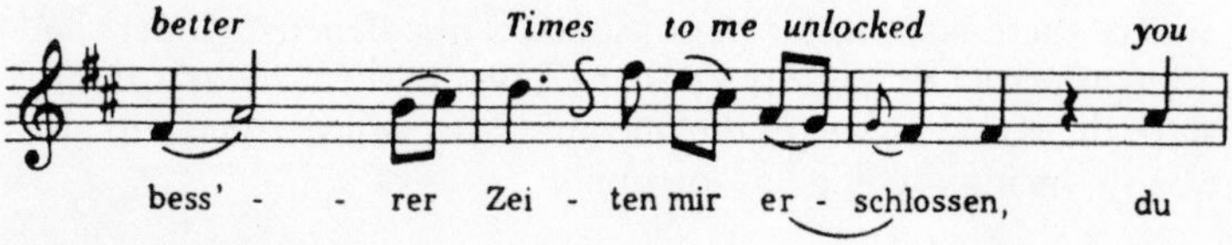

Sweep spaciously over this phrase.

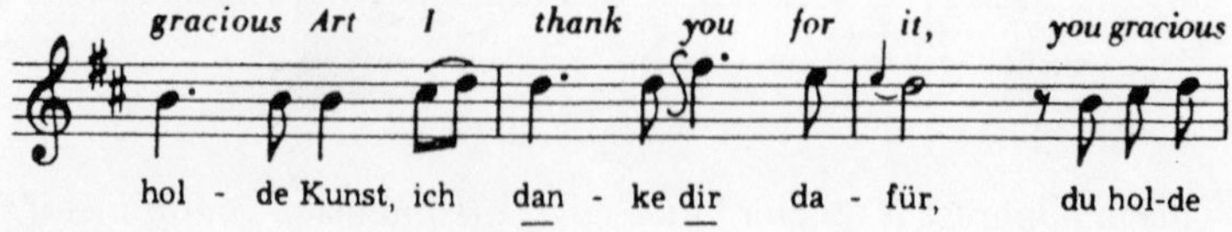

This 'i' vowel in 'dir' should be vibrant as in the word 'sing' — not squeezed.

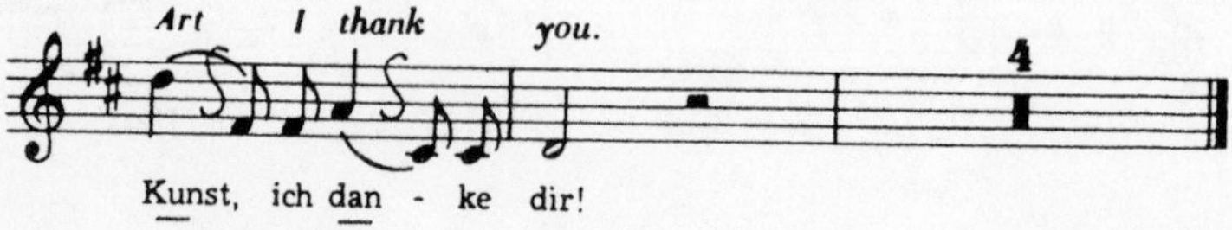

These two intervals on 'kunst' and 'danke' need careful linking. Come to rest with true sincerity and well centred vowels, and you will have energy to spare.